UNDERSTANDING HOMOSEXUALITY

UNDERSTANDING HOMOSEXUALITY

A Guide for Those Who
Know, Love, or Counsel
Gay and Lesbian
Individuals

Helen B. McDonald
and Audrey I. Steinhorn
Foreword by William Van Ornum

Crossroad • New York

1993

The Crossroad Publishing Company
370 Lexington Avenue
New York, NY 10017

Copyright © 1990 by Helen B. McDonald and Audrey I. Steinhorn
Foreword Copyright © 1990 by William Van Ornum

Printed in the United States of America

Library of Congress Cataloging-in-Publication Data

McDonald, Helen B.
    [Homosexuality]
    Understanding homosexuality : a guide for those who know, love, or
counsel gay and lesbian individuals / Helen B. McDonald and Audrey
I. Steinhorn ; foreword by William Van Ornum.
       p.   cm.
    Originally published: Homosexuality. New York : Continuum, 1990,
in series: The Continuum counseling series.
    Includes bibliographical references.
    ISBN 0-8245-1215-4 (pbk.)
    1. Homosexuality. 2. Gays—Counseling of. I. Steinhorn, Audrey
I. II. Title.
[RC558.M42 1993]
305.9'0664—dc20
                                             92-15506
                                              CIP

To my twin brother George (Scott) McDonald who introduced me to many wonderful gay men. His own personal struggle with AIDS taught me how valuable each moment in life can be.

—Helen B. McDonald

To my son Bart whose struggle with my homosexuality reminds me constantly that differences are hard, change is slow, and love is powerful. Our journey together, which at times has been painful, has enriched both our lives.

—Audrey I. Steinhorn

Contents

Foreword

Understanding Homosexuality

Friends, relatives, parents, and counselors will find *Understanding Homosexuality* informative and sensitive and a great help in understanding the sexual preferences of people who are homosexual.

One of the things that impressed me was the wide range of life-styles that represent homosexuality. The authors present numerous vignettes in the first chapter to convey that homosexuals live in all realms and strata of society. Even experienced counselors will learn from the variety of these cases.

In these days of AIDS awareness there may be a special sensitivity toward homosexuality, in some quarters becoming an irrational fear: homophobia. This book will do a great deal toward dispelling unrealistic notions and ideas as it presents, in a compassionate and balanced way, real-life issues with which many homosexual people struggle. The authors summarize issues that affect homosexuals along the lifespan. Theories of homosexuality, and common myths and misconceptions about these, are explored in detail. The process of "coming out," which can be traumatic and something to be worked through in counseling, is presented.

The role of religion and homosexuality is examined in a thorough manner, from looking at biblical passages and their contexts as they refer to homosexuality, to today's greater tolerance and acceptance of homosexuals as full members of particular churches and congregations. Readers with an interest in pastoral counseling will find this material especially interesting.

What happens when a married person with children discovers that he or she is homosexual? What happens when a homosexual couple decides that they would like to offer a family environment to a child? McDonald and Steinhorn look at the impact of homosexuality on the many dimensions of family life. The interaction of homosexuality and alcohol and substance abuse—of special importance now because of the increased chance of spreading AIDS (by not being careful and using "safer" sex procedures, or by sharing drug paraphernalia)—is also examined.

By reading this sensitive and compassionate book, the reader, whether pastor, psychologist, friend, social worker, or fellow community member, learns to see the full humanity in people whose identity is sometimes summarized as a proper noun *(Homosexuals)*. The authors bring a deep authenticity to this book, including many years devoted to counseling people who are struggling with gay and lesbian issues.

Filling in this detailed portrait are descriptions of "special groups" of gay men and lesbians, such as those living in rural areas, those who have a bisexual orientation, or those who are handicapped. There are also informative mentions of famous people who have been well known as gay.

Understanding Homosexuality is a book that will inspire the reader to pause and reflect on the many situations in life wherein a greater sensitivity to issues related to homosexuality would have been helpful. All readers will benefit from the compassionate and intelligent information that is provided by Helen McDonald and Audrey Steinhorn.

William Van Ornum, Ph.D.
Marist College
Poughkeepsie, New York

General Editor

Acknowledgments

The authorship of this book is shared by two people. The knowledge it reflects was acquired over many years and from many friends, clients, teachers, and therapists. This book represents a unique blending of our life experiences and would not have been composed as such if we were not life friends and partners. We see the book as a continuation of our learning processes.

We wish to thank William Van Ornum for approaching Audrey with the idea of writing a book on the subject of homosexuality. We appreciated his constant support and encouragement. His enthusiasm was contagious and especially helpful during times when we felt blocked.

Marion Howard and Dan Bloom (Daniel J.) donated much of their precious time and energy to read our manuscript. Their criticisms, questions, and suggestions were invaluable to our process. We cannot thank them enough.

In a class by herself is our dear friend Fumi Ukai who is responsible for all of our West Coast information. For ten years she has been cutting and clipping articles pertaining to gay and lesbian issues that she knew would be of interest to us. Many thanks go to her for all of her interest and support.

Other friends and colleagues also contributed to this project. Lucy Gilbert and Beverly Elkan shared their helpful ideas. Reverend Robert Davidson of the West Park Presbyterian Church in New York City loaned us some of his library. Alix Dobkin shared some of her personal resources concerning lesbian separatism and Michael Shernoff was our resource for some specific information pertaining to gay men.

We deeply appreciate the time and information William Arnold of the AIDS Related Community Services shared with us in updating the AIDS chapter for the paperback edition. Terry McGovern, director of the HIV Project of MFY Legal Service,

Incorporated, contributed invaluable information pertaining to women's HIV symptoms. Linda Harrington and Christina Spanos of Author-Author assisted us in updating the bibliography. Many thanks.

We wish to thank Penelope Boehm for coordinating the laborious tasks of editing and typing our manuscript. This was especially important since the writers are computer illiterate. Specific thanks go to David Boehm and John Dildine for their unique ability to edit our work to make sense out of what we had written in a way that maintained the integrity of our content. Additional thanks to John Dildine for typing the manuscript, and to Cornelia Brunner and Clarice Staff for their help with word processing.

Finally, we would like to thank each other. Finding time in already-busy schedules to write a book is difficult. Collaboration demands patience with cooperation as well as tolerance and respect for the other. Even though the subject matter is very important to us the writing process was at times tedious. The final result, however, was well worth the effort.

Authors' Note

The identities of the individuals in the case studies of this book have been carefully disguised in accordance with professional standards of confidentiality and in keeping with their rights to privileged communication with the authors.

UNDERSTANDING
HOMOSEXUALITY

1

Homosexuals Today

Today's homosexual community consists of as varied a group of people as you will find anywhere in our society. It is probably the most invisible minority group and one of the least understood. Most members of minorities have identifiable features such as color, age, sex, and various specific physical attributes. This is not true of homosexuals. They come in all shapes, ages, colors, and sizes. They work at various jobs, in different professions, and come from diverse religious and socioeconomic backgrounds.

Many lesbians and gay men are well adjusted and lead successful lives just as many heterosexual people do. Some are politicians like Congressman Barney Frank of Massachusetts. Others are contemporary writers like Rita Mae Brown *(Rubyfruit Jungle)*, Edmund White *(The Beautiful Room Is Empty)*, Adrienne Rich *(Of Women Born)*, and Audre Lorde *(The Cancer Journals)*. Bessie Smith and Liberace are famous in the music world. Famous people associated with the theater and film industries are Rock Hudson and Tennessee Williams. Gertrude Stein and Alice B. Toklas, E. M. Forster, W. H. Auden, James Baldwin, and Walt Whitman are famous in the world of literature.

Many people believe that homosexuals are easily identifiable. For example, that a male homosexual (gay man) is a "pretty, swishy, immaculately groomed, effeminate man." A female homosexual (lesbian) has "short hair, wears jeans and men's shirts, and has a tough, masculine air about her." While it is true that some lesbians and gay men do fit these stereotypes, there are many heterosexual people who do also. Stereotypes, or prejudgments do exist for all groups, but they only refer to a small segment of the group and say nothing about who those people really are.

17

In the following pages we will give you an idea of who some of these people really are. The descriptions represent only a few of the gay and lesbian people you might encounter. We would like you to familiarize yourself with them as they are referred to later in various examples throughout the book.

One group that people seldom think of as being lesbian or gay is found in our older population. This is quite understandable, as many of our elders do not identify themselves as lesbian or gay. They often tend to see or refer to their life partners of ten, fifteen, and twenty years or more as their dear friends/roommates. This is not surprising when we stop to think of the homophobia that existed twenty to thirty years ago—before the "Stonewall" uprising that took place in New York in 1969, when the gay liberation movement began. Frequently gay men and lesbians were thought to be crazy. They were ostracized, hospitalized in mental wards, and sent to psychiatrists to be "straightened" out. As a result of such terrorizing homophobia, many of them repressed their homosexuality.

Lillian, a writer, is an elderly Protestant woman who has lived "in the closet" (see glossary) all of her life with her roommate of twenty years, Mary. She resides in a small town in the Midwest where she once was a high school teacher. As "dear friends," Lillian and Mary never refer to their relationship as being lesbian or homosexual. They lead a quiet, inconspicuous life and tend to socialize primarily with other women. People in their community consider them to be sweet and friendly "old maids" and feel sorry for them because they never married.

Lillian has diabetes and a heart problem and has been hospitalized a few times for these conditions. She and Mary have had several excruciatingly painful experiences when Lillian was in the hospital, because their relationship was not recognized as legitimate by the hospital staff.

Lillian and Mary live with a constant worry that the medical staff will never acknowledge Mary as having either the ability and/or the authority to make decisions about Lillian's care, should she not be able to do it for herself. Having internalized the homophobia of their generation and learned and practiced for many years the passive female gender role behavior they were expected to exhibit, Lillian and Mary were used to never "making waves." It would never occur to them to speak up about anything that would draw attention to themselves and especially their relationship.

One group that tends to be of concern to everyone is the adolescents, since teenagers go through such turbulent times in their efforts to discover who they are—especially in the area of their sexual development and identity formation. Adolescence is a time when it is age-appropriate for the youth to "hang out" in same sex groups and to have one or two very close friends of the same gender. It is a time of heightened sexual feelings, anxieties and confusion—what are these feelings all about and what do you do with them? It is a time when it is also of utmost importance to be similar to one's friends and to belong to the group regardless of one's cultural background. Having anything different about one's self or one's family can be experienced with great pain, discomfort, embarrassment, or a deep sense of shame.

Luis is an adolescent Latino male from a small Southwestern town who has had sexual feelings and thoughts about other males, but has never acted on them. The object of much ridicule, which has become increasingly intolerable to him, Luis has thought of running away from home to a large city. Fear and a desire not to hurt his family have kept him from leaving.

Although he is not particularly effeminate, some of Luis's peers tease him about his lack of "machismo." They have started to wonder about his sexuality because he does not seem to be as excited about girls as they are and has not had many girlfriends. They also think it odd that he rarely talks about girls and that he keeps to himself so much. In a culture where machismo is *"muy importante,"* Luis just does not measure up, and he knows it. This knowledge is causing him increasing anxiety. Knowing no one like him, he has kept his frightening thoughts a secret and has tried to act as "normal" as possible. This has been causing him great strain. Luis thinks he knows only one other boy who may feel as he does about males, but he has never dared to raise the topic with him. Basically, he feels like the only gay adolescent in the world—a lonely spot indeed. (This is a common adolescent gay experience.)

Luis's mother is worried about him because he always seems to be alone. She keeps telling him to talk to the youth worker at the community center. Luis agrees in order to pacify his mother, but never goes for help because he believes that a man has to take care of his own problems. He secretly fears being told that he is sick and worries about being made fun of by everyone, including the youth worker.

As a senior in high school with a good academic record who wants very much to save face, Luis has begun to talk about his ideas of leaving town and moving to a big city once he graduates. He knows this would be acceptable to his parents, since they have relatives in the city where he is planning to move. He could earn money there and even consider the option of continuing his education in the evening. Luis is most excited about the possibility of exploring his sexuality further in a setting that might be more supportive to him and where he hopes to meet other people struggling with the same questions.

For many lesbians and gay men, religion has been and continues to be a significant part of their lives, despite the fact that most religious teachings tend to consider homosexuality a sin and/or an abomination. Although there are religious groups (Dignity, Integrity, gay synagogues, etc.) that offer services to lesbians and gay men, these are not necessarily recognized by the officials of those churches. The groups have been formed to help their lesbian and gay members struggle with the conflicts that arise between their sexual orientation and the teachings of their church or organized religion. This conflict has at times caused lesbians and gay men to feel isolated from their religious communities.

Sylvia is a twenty-five-year-old white Lutheran woman who lives in a small town in the Midwest, where she works as a bank teller. As a valued employee, Sylvia has been able to take advantage of the bank's educational incentives and has completed several courses at a nearby college. She already has received two promotions and is looking forward to a third.

Sylvia and her lover of three years, Jane, share an apartment in town. Although Sylvia's parents want nothing to do with her because of her sexual orientation, she is still close to her three siblings, whom she sees regularly.

Sylvia is very happy in her relationship with Jane. They are part of a group of women who meet once a month at each other's homes for pot luck suppers and much needed talking and sharing of personal experiences. This group also provides parties and weekend outings to gay resort areas, political activities, etc. Since Sylvia and Jane are not "out" to many people, the gatherings provide an important social outlet. They are quite isolated and look forward to any contact with other lesbians.

Sylvia has struggled very deeply and has experienced many emotional upheavals on her journey to explore her sexual orientation. To help her with her feelings she sought out pastoral counseling with an interfaith minister and has done extensive reading on the topic. She often attends gay services at a church in a nearby large city that has also been helping her reconcile her religious beliefs with her sexual orientation.

Sylvia misses her parents and hopes that in time they will be able to reconnect with her. In recognition of the pain that they are experiencing in their own isolation, she periodically sends them literature about a local group of parents of lesbians and gay men.

Many people assume that lesbians and gay men are single and have never been married to a person of the opposite sex. This is another stereotype, however, and is not true. As a matter of fact, a large number of gay men and lesbians have been married or are married today. Some people are unaware of their homosexuality or bisexuality until after they have been married and had children. Others make a conscious choice to hide their homosexual or bisexual identity in favor of the more socially accepted and respected heterosexual relationship, have children, and later are not able to continue the "straight masquerade." Some people remain in their marriage even after their homosexual or bisexual awareness develops and lead a double life because of their fears about coming out and possibly losing everything that is important to them. Others come out to their spouses and get divorced or live together with the understanding that either could be involved with someone else. The process of discovering that one is lesbian or gay when one is married is most typically a painful, frightening, and yet often growth-producing experience.

Isaiah is a forty-seven-year-old black gay lawyer who lives in a large Eastern city. He became aware of his homosexual orientation in his late thirties, but did not come out to his wife or children. Before he could do this, Isaiah first needed to deal with his own fears of losing his children and of being ostracized or rejected, not only by his family, but also by the members of his profession and the black community within which he lived and worked.

Although he is still not "out" professionally, Isaiah has shared the information with his family. He and his wife, Florence, have tried to deal with the problems his new identity has caused, but it has proved to be very difficult for them both. This was especially true when Isaiah got involved with another man. It was at that point that his wife asked for and got a divorce. Isaiah was open with his grown children about the reasons for the divorce and also about his male lover. His son was very hurt and threatened by the information and discontinued all contact with his father. His daughter, who had made several lesbian and gay friends in college, was initially upset but became more understanding and supportive of her father as time passed.

Isaiah is very content in his relationship with Don, a court reporter he met during one of his trials. They have both become active in civil and gay rights causes. Isaiah is sad about his son's rejection of him, but he knows it is unfair to expect his son to accept the news about his homosexuality right away, since he himself was unable to do so. He realizes that his son has to mourn the loss of the person he thought his father was. Although hurt, Isaiah realizes this is a process his son has to go through at his own pace.

Numerous lesbian and gay male couples value family life and children and often form alternative families of their own. There is a common belief that lesbians and gay men choose the life style of a homosexual because they dislike children and/or are physically unable to reproduce. The question of whether or not one likes children or being a parent has nothing at all to do with being lesbian or gay. This is another stereotype—the assumption is that all heterosexuals like children and that gay people do not. The fact is that there are some who do and some who do not in both groups. As for reproduction, the person whom you choose to be sexual with has nothing to do with your reproductive organs or the ability to reproduce. Lesbian eggs are receptive to sperm from both heterosexual and gay males while gay males can be sperm donors for both heterosexual and lesbian women. However, the frequency of the use of gay male sperm has decreased since AIDS. Many lesbians and gay men go to great lengths to consciously plan the birth of their children—be it through intercourse or through alternative insemination. When unable to have their own children, adoptions and foster parenting are other options frequently explored.

Contrary to the more traditional heterosexual family, the biological gay father usually does not live with his child. Some men may be just sperm donors, some may be minimally involved, while others are very active, often participating in planning the child's life course, contributing to his/her financial support, and having his/her child for regular visits.

Karen and Carol are a lesbian couple who reside in a large West Coast city. Both in their early thirties, they have been together for five years. Carol is a social worker in a large municipal hospital and Karen works as a nutritionist at a private nursing home on a part-time basis. Karen's schedule allows her to be home more during the day to be with their one-year-old son, Greg. Carol, Greg's biological mother, became pregnant through planned intercourse with a long-time high school friend, Bill, who was interested in fathering a child. Bill, who has been aware of his homosexuality since adolescence, lives alone and shares daytime childcare with Karen since his work schedule as a writer provides flexibility. Greg seems to be a happy child who thrives on loving care given by the three primary adults in his life.

Karen's parents were very upset when they first heard of Carol's pregnancy. Although they accepted their daughter's lesbianism, they were concerned about her rights as a nonbiological parent. One of their older children had recently been divorced and involved in a complex child-custody suit. This raised their awareness of the problems inherent in the breaking up of a family unit. They have been a little reluctant to get involved with Greg, due to their own fears of possibly losing a grandchild should anything every happen to Karen and Carol's relationship. They also worry about Bill's role. They worry that Greg may be gay because his father is—another stereotype! However they are glad that he is so involved in the baby's care at present.

In planning for the baby's conception and birth, Karen, Carol, and Bill consulted with a lawyer in order to spell out and protect, as much as possible, everyone's rights. They drew up both a "donor agreement" for Bill and a "nomination of a guardian for a minor" agreement for Karen. Altogether the three devised and signed a partnership agreement that clarified their intent to provide jointly for and nurture their child even in the event that they were no longer living together in the family home.

Although Greg is just a baby, all three parents talk regularly about the problems they have and/or expect to encounter as Greg gets older. These include what they will tell Greg, what they will tell the schools, how they will help Greg deal with peers from heterosexual families, etc. The three parents know they cannot anticipate all the problems involved in raising their child, but they are ready to deal with them like any other parent who takes on the responsibility of bringing a child into the world.

No one would disagree that AIDS—Acquired Immune Deficiency Syndrome—is the most significant public health problem of the decade. Many men, women, and children have suffered or will suffer from the effects of this ravaging disease in one form or another. They will come down with a variety of infections, such as pneumocystis carini pneumonia (PCP), Kaposi's Sarcoma, toxoplasmosis, cryptococcal meningitis, etc.

Often the initial symptoms present themselves in the form of night sweats, diarrhea, cough, enlarged lymph glands, fatigue, fever, and weight loss. A disease complex that depresses the immune system, AIDS used to kill its victims within eighteen to twenty-four months after symptoms had begun to present themselves. It is increasingly becoming more of a chronic manageable disease, although the prognosis for long-term survival is poor.

Feelings of terror, guilt, shame, and/or hopelessness typically occur when a person with AIDS first learns of his/her diagnosis. Following this, denial often takes place because of the stigma associated with the disease, the fear of being rejected by one's peers, family, and/or society as a whole, and the fear of losing one's life.

John is a forty-one-year-old designer who lives in New York City. He and his lover, Harry, own a large co-op apartment on the west side of town and attend the gay synagogue regularly. Although John and Harry know of several people who have died of AIDS, none of their close friends have come down with the disease. They never expected that either of them would get it. They have considered themselves monogamous during their seven years together, although each has been sexual outside the relationship on a few occasions following major upheavals in their lives.

It was during their vacation on Fire Island that John first began to complain about a slight fever, fatigue, and soreness under the arms. Neither took his symptoms seriously, because they both knew how exhausted he was from his busy work and social schedule. It was not until John started having night sweats that he and Harry decided to consult a doctor.

The doctor thought John might have a flu, but decided to take blood samples to test for the presence of HIV antibodies, because he knew from what John had shared with him that John had not always practiced safer sex. The tests came back positive. Both men were shocked and immediately wondered who was to blame. This caused a serious disruption in their relationship, until they finally realized it was a moot point. Anxiety remained as to whether or not John would develop AIDS.

For the next several months John appeared healthy, although the fever and fatigue persisted, along with sporadic diarrhea. He and Harry decided not to tell anyone, because of their fear of negative responses. They did not even tell other gay friends. Since none of their close friends had come down with AIDS, they could not anticipate how they would react. Their own fears were so great that they did not dare to take any chances. Then John began to have severe night sweats along with a hacking cough. He became dehydrated and was admitted to the hospital. Tests revealed the presence of PCP.

John and Harry decided that it was time to tell their friends and family what was really going on. For them it was another "coming out" process. Although both families knew of their son's relationships they did not really know anything about AIDS and were subsequently shocked at the news. Although they accepted their son's homosexual relationship, the parents' fear of the stigma attached to AIDS prevented them from discussing it with their friends.

There are some people who see themselves as having made a conscious choice to become a lesbian or gay man—their homosexuality did not just "happen" to them. Their choice has been based on sexual, social, emotional, or political reasons. Some lesbians feel the presence of men limits their creativity, spontaneity, and imagination. They avoid men not because of a dislike of them, but rather because they find that an environment of all women provides more of an opportunity for increased creative growth and development.

Some people make the choice because they do not like members of the opposite sex and identify themselves as separatists— refusing to socialize in the presence of the opposite sex. Some even refuse to be in groups that include children of the opposite sex who may be over the age of nine or ten.

Politically, many women choose to remain separate as a way to avoid dealing with their oppression by male power. Emotionally some men and women just prefer affectionate ties with members of their own sex. Socially, some men and women prefer being with their own kind, in same sex clubs or discos where they are free from the constraints of the sexist (or heterosexist) roles society typically expects of them.

Gail, a thirty-year-old printer, lives in a West Coast city. She is single by choice, but has a very active social life. She decided to become a lesbian in her early twenties during a period of radical political activity. She lives communally with four other women. She has considered becoming pregnant and bearing a child, but is concerned about giving birth to a male child even though the other women in the house offered to help her raise a baby.

Gail works hard at her job. Since printing is an activity usually thought of as men's work, she is under a lot of pressure on the job from her male fellow workers. Gail also plays hard. Since her social life takes place primarily in women's bars, she has begun to notice an increase in her alcohol consumption. Once she was able to limit herself to two drinks an evening, but now she sets no limits at all. Several times Gail has blacked out, having no recollection of the events of the evening. She often has been told that she was verbally abusive to her friends, and she has been noticing that they are becoming reluctant to go out with her anymore.

Several friends have suggested that Gail go to see a counselor or go to Alcoholics Anonymous meetings. Gail is now beginning to think her problem is serious, but is afraid to go for help. She is concerned about whether she would be accepted as a lesbian. She does not know of any lesbian counselors and is afraid to walk into an AA meeting alone.

Gary is a fifty-year-old, celibate (since the appearance of AIDS in the gay male community), effeminate male who hates women. He owns his own bookstore in Chicago and caters his books to the male taste. He belongs to a fairy circle and has made a lot of friends through his association with it.

He is a wonderful cook who has never lived with a lover, yet has had many relationships. He has no living family members, as is true for many older lesbians and gay men. He makes his gay group his family. He spends his vacations and all the major holidays with them.

Gary has lost many dear friends to AIDS and is concerned that he will be alone in his later years. He is starting to get more in touch with his spiritual side and is examining the meaning of life and death. He is considering joining a study group that is run by a gay minister for members of his church's homosexual community.

Perhaps the most isolated people within the lesbian and gay communities are those who have either mental or physical disabilities. These people are doubly stigmatized. They are not considered "whole" and they are not considered to be heterosexual people. They are isolated for a variety of reasons. Some people are isolated because many of the places they would like to go are physically inaccessible. Many are also isolated because of their negative self-image and low self-esteem, which often existed before they became aware of the fact that they were homosexual. Some people are disabled from birth and some people, like Eddie, acquired their disability later in life.

Eddie is a white Anglo-Saxon gay man who is thirty years old. He lives in a suburb of the Twin Cities in Minnesota. Eddie recently moved back into his own apartment, which had been modified for his use. The modifications included, among other things, the widening of doorways, the lowering of sinks and closets, and the installation of bars in the bathroom to facilitate Eddie's bathing and toileting. Eddie needed these modifications because a year ago he became a paraplegic as a result of a car accident. After leaving the hospital, Eddie had gone to a rehabilitation center for physical therapy and the acquisition of new skills.

Eddie is a successful stockbroker. Because of this, he was able to finance the alterations to his apartment. Although he looked forward to leaving the rehab center, Eddie was frightened to be going home on his own. He wasn't sure if he could manage by himself. A few of his friends had volunteered to "help" him, but he wasn't sure what kind of help he needed. Eddie wished that Larry, his ex-lover, was around. Larry had had a great deal of trouble accepting Eddie with his new disability, and had left him. Eddie was very angry and hurt by this. He was also concerned about ever getting a new lover. "After all, who could love a cripple?" he wondered. Eddie was having significant difficulty accepting his changed body. Since he didn't accept it, he couldn't imagine how anyone else could.

Prior to his accident, Eddie had been an extremely active person. He jogged, rode a bicycle, skied, and worked out at the gym. He knew how much value his gay male friends placed on physical fitness and attractiveness. Eddie could not imagine anything attractive about his "dead" legs and his wheelchair. Although they had talked a great deal about sexual functioning at the rehab center, Eddie was most afraid about his ability to make love with another man and concerned that no man would ever want to make love with him. Eddie had been quite a "stud" before and now whenever he was not able to have or sustain an erection he became panic-stricken.

Eddie's social worker at the hospital had led a group for the patients on his floor, which he found very helpful but isolating because everyone else was heterosexual. Eddie would like to join a gay disabled group but he doesn't know where to begin to look for one.

The preceding vignettes have been presented as a means of introducing the reader to a sampling of members of the lesbian and gay community and problems and issues that occur in their lives. Some of these problems occur because the issues are universal to all people and others only because the people depicted are not heterosexual and are therefore seen as different. Homophobia creates isolation, alienation, loneliness, as well as lack of support and community. In the following chapters we will explore some of these issues and problems in depth and discuss techniques counselors can utilize in working with these clients.

2

What Do You Mean You Are Not Heterosexual?

A s you can see from the cameos in the first chapter, many lesbians and gay men do not appear to be that different from other people you encounter in your everyday life. Many of you think that you have never met a lesbian or a gay man. In fact, you have probably met many people who are lesbian or gay, but they have not let you know it.

The primary reason for this is that homosexuality can go unnoticed. Most heterosexuals do not openly talk to strangers about their sexual desires and partners. This is even more true of lesbians and gay men, and this reticence makes sense when we consider how much the public perception of one's sexuality matters in our society.

Another reason you may not know many gay people is due to homophobia. Homophobia is an irrational fear of homosexuals or a fear of one's own real or potential homosexuality. This fear applies to homosexuals and nonhomosexuals alike. Most of us have grown up hearing negative remarks made about homosexuals. We all know many of the derogatory terms used to describe people who are lesbian or gay, such as dyke, faggot, queer, fairy, lesbo, etc.

People have used these terms, either as a way to hurt and demean others, to appease fears and create distance between themselves and others, or as a way to appear "big and tough" in the eyes of people they might want to impress. Some people have had the painful experience of having those words used to describe themselves, whether they were gay or not. All of us have learned that a lesbian or gay man is an outcast, even if we do not know what the words mean. We do know in no uncertain terms, that we do not want to be called these names. The pain of being the object of homophobia is a very real reason for hiding certain information about ourselves.

A third reason that many people think they have never met a gay man or lesbian has to do with the stereotypes mentioned in chapter 1. Since many people use stereotypical behavior to define what a homosexual is, they never imagine that someone whom they see as a "whole person" might be gay.

Yet, despite the many pressures, there are many lesbians and gay men in our society. How often does it happen? According to Kinsey's famous study on sexuality, approximately 10 percent of the population will be homosexual.[1] Does that mean that, on the average, one person out of ten in every family will be homosexual? It's hard to know for several reasons. One is that many homosexual people are still "in the closet" and even close family members do not know about their homosexuality. Another is that no factors have been identified that might predict how many children in a family will be lesbian or gay or help guarantee the production of heterosexual children. After all, most gay people have straight parents.

Before we proceed further it is important that we comment on bisexuality. Bisexuality refers to people who are attracted emotionally and sexually to people of either gender. Bisexuality is considered by some to be as valid a sexual orientation as homosexuality or heterosexuality. Some people consider it a phase, while others do not even acknowledge its existence. Why are some people considered bisexual? The truth is that we do not know—just as we do not know what makes a person homosexual or heterosexual.

Some people believe that bisexuals relate socially and emotionally to both a man and a woman at the same time. This is not necessarily so. Having the capacity to relate to both genders does not mean that one does, since bisexuals—like all of us—can enter into a whole variety of relationships, or none at all. Some bisexuals never become involved with both sexes, while others do. The key to how one identifies one's self is to be found in self-perception. There is no one set of behaviors that would serve as a test to indicate whether one is or is not bisexual.

There are many different ideas and theories that have been

put forth over the years. One idea holds that homosexuals are simply "born that way." Another theory reasons that gay men and lesbians have "weak genes." Others propose that the cause is a developmental lag. A few suggest that homosexual behavior may result from hormone patterns that are different from those in heterosexual men and women.

Prior to the mid–nineteenth century, homosexuality was seen primarily as a sin. Then, because of changes in society, certain behaviors that had previously been seen to be religious issues were slowly taken over by the sciences, and a sinful unnatural act gradually came to be referred to as an illness. Homosexuality then came to be considered a mental illness. Most people have heard the words weird, crazy, deviant, pervert, queer, and pathological applied to homosexual people. These labels are a legacy from that time.

As K. P. Johanns writes, "For the past year-and-a-half I was a prisoner (I mean 'patient') at Marlboro State Hospital in New Jersey. Ten days ago I was released, and a year-and-a-half of hell came to an end."[2]

She explained, "At age eleven I tried to commit suicide, and was placed in a private hospital. After I got out I became more aware of my gay feelings and came out to my mother at age fourteen or fifteen. That didn't go over very well. . . .

"I kept crying to myself, 'Isn't there a woman who can love and accept me?' Several hospitalizations ensued, once with shock therapy. All this time the shrinks were trying to 'cure' me. I couldn't take that. Everyone threw up their hands in disgust at this flipped out dyke. I was heavily medicated—that was the only way the place was tolerable. My lesbianism was violently repressed."

Some believe that the personalities of the parent couple affect the development of the child's sexual orientation. For example, there is a widespread belief that a male will become gay if he has a strong mother and a weak father. However, in our experience most families like this have straight children. Interestingly, the corollary of a strong father and a weak mother for lesbians does not seem to exist. Some believe a child becomes homosexual because the parent of the opposite sex has been cruel to them. For example, they believe that a girl may become a lesbian because her father was excessively mean to or incestuous with her.

Some even believe that homosexuality is contagious and can be "caught" by being around a lesbian or gay man. We all know that parents fear their boy or girl may become a homosexual if the child has a lesbian or gay teacher. We also know that most young people and even some adults fear they may become gay or lesbian if they hang around friends of theirs who are homosexual. These fears are based on a broader belief that everyone is born heterosexual, but some people become homosexual as a result of being seduced by an older homosexual. No evidence exists to support these fears, which are based on lack of knowledge. This is another stereotype, as well as a pernicious prejudice.

Another belief is that homosexual behavior is just an expression of rebellion by children toward their parents. The implication is that by not conforming, the "child" (who can be any age) is trying to get back at the parents for some hurt he/she has experienced in the past. Although this may occasionally be true, it is not the norm.

It is not the authors' intent to do an in-depth study of the various theories and beliefs about what causes homosexuality. Rather it is our intent to help the reader become open to the fact that there are many theories and to be aware of what some of them are. No one knows what "causes" homosexuality or bisexuality, just as no one knows what "causes" heterosexuality. Sexual development is various.

Although no one reason can be cited for sure, many ideas and beliefs have been presented over the years and continue to be put forth today *as if they are the truth*. We all know that people believe what they want to believe.

Some of you readers will have heard of ideas or theories that are not being presented here simply because the authors are not familiar with them. This is an important example of what can happen when people are presented with situations involving others who are different from them. In trying to understand the differences, people—you and I—tend to use our own life experience as a basis for our understanding. Therefore, what may be a widespread belief in one part of the country may not even be known in another area, or even to a different group of people.

In thinking about theories on origins of homosexuality, it is important for the counselor—for everyone—to try to understand what their own beliefs are. This is so that your own biases will not interfere in the work. The question for all of us is to find out how open we can be, especially in view of the fact that society is so closed.

When we begin working with our clients, we have to accept them as they are. This includes accepting what they believe. For example, a client may come to you in a great rage at his parents for "making him gay," or a client may come in and talk about there being something wrong with him/her. Is there something clinically wrong, or are they just different? The *DSM III-R* (1989) places homosexuality in the category of "Other Sexual Disorder Not Otherwise Specified," when there is "persistent and marked distress" about one's sexual orientation.[3]

It is not the counselor's job to change people's beliefs, but it is our job to help them see as much as possible that other options and choices may be available to them. As counselors we help people deal with the pain and the problems that come from their belief system. But our most important job is to help people accept who they are. This means that we will need to help lesbians and gay men accept the fact that they are different. Once they are able to accept this, they may very well find that their sexual orientation is contrary to their own belief system. At this point, some may decide that although they experience themselves as lesbian or gay, they will choose to live the life-style of a heterosexual because the alternative is too painful. For example, a married woman decides to remain with her husband and children after she has had several affairs with women. She bases her decision to remain on her religious beliefs that value marriage and family and consider homosexuality to be a sin. In another situation, a man decides to marry his fiancée in the hope that this commitment will take away his interest in men. He may have been brought up to believe that bisexuality and homosexuality are totally unacceptable and abnormal, and he may be deathly afraid of being rejected by his family and friends.

Some may decide to "stay in the closet"—to keep their homosexuality a secret. A man or woman becomes aware of his/her homosexuality, does not tell his/her spouse, and practices in secret. Others will decide that, in order for them to feel fulfilled in their lives, they must pursue the life-style of a lesbian or gay man and be as open as possible. For example, some people's homophobia initially causes them to deny the significance of their interest in people of the same sex. In their denial they may choose love objects of the opposite sex who, for one reason or the other, would never be good marital partners. Meanwhile they start to make gay friends and become more aware of their true selves. This awareness can make them feel good. Eventually many find it intolerable to continue to stay in the closet. They find that the closet leaves them very isolated and feeds into the sense that there is something wrong with them. They feel like second-class citizens, especially when friends and colleagues talk about their own weekend activities, who their current lover is, or whom they have socialized with; the person in the closet can only speak in generalities. Most typically closet homosexuals will develop a way of presenting themselves to others that protects them from being asked what they have done. Often they will not even be included in such conversations.

For example:

MARY. John and I had a great time last night. We went out and had a scrumptious dinner at a French restaurant. Then we went to the theater and saw a great show. Then we went dancing.

GENE. That's great! Nancy and I had a boring time. We stayed home and watched TV. And watched TV. And watched TV. There were no sports on. I can't tell you how much I hate sitcoms.

JANICE. Oh, Gene, that's pathetic. Maurice and I took a walk along Columbus Avenue and pretended that we each had a thousand dollars to spend.

CAROL. What a wonderful idea—you two must have had so much fun!

JANICE. We really did. Joe, what did you do last night?

JOE. I studied for the exam I am taking tomorrow.

GENE. Well, what did Sandra do while you were studying?

JOE. She tried to be real quiet. She knows how important this exam is to me.

CAROL. That's just like her. She's always thinking about other people.

JOE. You know, Carol, that's really true. That's one of the things I love most about her. By the way, what did you do last night?

CAROL. Not much.

JANICE. Hey, who wants to go for a drink after work?

MARY. I'd love to, but John and I have plans to meet another couple.

JOE. I have to study.

GENE. Sorry, I'm going to a basketball game with Nancy.

CAROL. (Says nothing.)

JANICE. Oh well, maybe another time.

It is important for us as counselors to realize that any choice a client makes is valid, extremely difficult to make, and typically very painful for the person making it. The belief that homosexuality is a very undesirable attribute continues to prevent many lesbians and gay men from tuning in to themselves. It has also kept many who think of themselves as being homosexual from sharing this insight with their friends and family. Because they do not want to be seen as insulting, many nongays may not ask questions or otherwise raise the issue of homosexuality with their reticent friends or clients.

How many of you make a point of including questions about same sex interests or pursuits in your intake procedure? How many hesitate to ask specific questions about sexual orientation, even after you have seen someone for a period of time, and have begun to get pieces of information that indicate possible lesbian or gay interests? How many of you even think to listen for information that might imply nonheterosexuality?

These are very important questions to ask of oneself. They can help you get in touch with your own homophobia, which you may not have been fully aware of. They are also very important because lesbians and gay men may try to test the counselor by dropping clues. Remember, most homosexual clients will not trust you with this special information, at least not right away, because of their strong fears of a negative response and eventual rejection. Here, it should be noted that a lack of response by the counselor can be interpreted as negative because silence can imply that the listener is either too uncomfortable or too uninterested to respond.

Sometimes the pain that the client experiences while exploring his/her sexual and emotional orientation is so great that the counselor may be tempted to shut him/her down. For example, your client is experiencing great anguish about being teased and kidded over her 5 foot 10 inch height and her very tomboyish ways. Boys will play basketball with her, but not ask her for a date. She is very conscious of her attraction to other females and terrified that people will discover her secret. She cannot tell her parents because she is afraid the information will "kill" them. She fears that her friends will laugh at her, label her weird, and ostracize her. She feels desperately alone, lonely, and scared.

This is enough pain and fear to overwhelm anyone including the counselor. We may be tempted to calm the client by trying to look at positives, rather than helping him/her explore further. Who wants more pain?

Actually what we often do not realize is that our own sense of being personally overwhelmed is very similar to what our friend or client is going through. If we are able to perceive ourselves in this way, then we will be able to tune in to our client's feelings and help him/her. Saying to this frightened client in the example above, "It must be terribly lonely and frightening to be in your situation," communicates that you realize how overwhelmed she feels, and can be a step in breaking down her sense of isolation.

One big question at this time is whether the person is really lesbian or gay or bisexual. Often the counselor can become anxious about influencing the client to adopt or abandon the view that he/she is homosexual or bisexual. Here it is important for you to realize that, although you do have the power to help a client be freer to explore his or her sexuality, you do not have the power to determine it. The most important thing is to tune in to where the client is at, while always paying attention to your own biases and anxieties and how they might interfere in your client's process.

3

Come Out, Come Out, Wherever You Are

$\mathbf{M}$any of you may have heard the phrase "coming out" or "coming out of the closet" and wondered what it means. Coming out—as defined by the authors—is a lifelong process that all people experience when they allow themselves and/or others to discover who they really are. The term refers in particular to those aspects which are the most difficult for the individual and others to accept. The process can begin at any time in one's life.

Most typically, coming out refers to the process that lesbians and gay men go through when they discover that they are attracted to and prefer to have intimate relationships with people of the same sex. They deal with it every time they make new friends, when they change jobs, when they think about having children, when they buy a house, when they go to the hospital, when they choose a therapist, etc. It is even an issue for the elderly, whom one seldom thinks of as being lesbian or gay. What will the response of the nursing home be if their sexual preference is known? What about a retirement community—will they be well received? Coming out is a process that is both very frightening and very exciting to the person who is going through it.

Coming out is a time when a person focuses on the ways in which he/she differs from the mainstream of the population. It is a time when one can feel very much alone, because old supports do not work and new ones are not in place yet. It is an odd time because just as one is discovering something very special about him/herself, he/she is also frightened that others will become privy to this knowledge and reject him/her. It is also an odd time because while the person is gaining a new sense of self, he/she is simultaneously losing an old sense of self-identity. Suddenly what one always thought his/her life would be like is put to question. Things one expected to do are seen in a new perspective.

For example, the dream of having a child is very different for the homosexual than for the heterosexual. The plan to go to graduate school can become more complicated if one feels that he/she could be rejected because of this newly perceived identity. Typically, coming out is a time in a homosexual's life when paranoia becomes paramount. Yet, it has been said that there is often some reality in paranoia. Being lesbian or gay is risky business in our society and it is not being paranoid to acknowledge this. Coming out then is a period of transition which, once begun, lasts a lifetime.

In the past ten to fifteen years various writers have presented their views on the coming-out process. Although there is variation in these models, the examples the different writers present share certain elements in common. For example—the initial phase of coming out usually involves a conscious or preconscious awareness. The second phase involves various forms of exploration and acknowledgment. A third phase involves various aspects of acceptance. The final phase of coming out is devoted to the integration of newly formed relationships, both with peers and with intimates.

One writer, Vivien Cass[1] has described the following six stages: confusion, comparison, tolerance, acceptance, pride, and synthesis.

To help understand what this process might look like we will apply Cass's stages to the case of Sylvia, the bank teller first described in chapter 1.

Confusion—As an adolescent Sylvia began to suspect that something was "wrong" with her. She realized with much bewilderment that she was attracted to females, rather than to males.

Comparison—Sylvia felt very different from others and very alone. She tried to deny her feelings and became very flirtatious with young men in her class. She dated as often as possible.

Tolerance—When Sylvia began her banking courses at the local college, she met some lesbians and gay men. She was very relieved to find out that they were no more weird than most of the heterosexual people she knew. Although she did not see herself as lesbian, Sylvia participated with groups of lesbians in various activities in an effort to make new friends and see what lesbians were like as people.

Acceptance—As Sylvia made new lesbian and gay friends she became more aware of how comfortable she was in their company. She even found herself attracted to a particular woman and began having fantasies about getting involved with her. She stopped dating men and saw less and less of her old crowd. She began a lesbian sexual relationship.

Pride—Sylvia preferred to be in the company of lesbians and consciously sought out conferences, literature, and social events that focused on lesbian and gay issues. She became more aware of the various ways in which homophobia presented itself in everyday life situations. In her frustration and anger, she joined a local gay activist group and got herself on the mailing list of several national gay political groups in an effort to become more involved.

Despite her increasing pride in her new identity as a lesbian, Sylvia only felt free to "come out" in a few situations with carefully selected people. She did not want to repeat the traumatic experience she had had with her parents who rejected her once she made her sexual preference known.

Synthesis—As Sylvia became more comfortable with her life as a lesbian, she slowly started to renew contact with some of her old heterosexual friends. She was selective about whom she would share her new awareness with. She began monthly attendance at gay church services in a nearby large city.

Despite her parents' initial rejection, Sylvia hoped that time would help them become reconciled to the loss of the daughter they once thought they knew. She tried not to be angry with them, even though her sense of hurt was very deep. With help from her pastoral counselor, she saw their rejection as a form of mourning. Sylvia deepened her relationships with her siblings, who knew about and accepted her lesbianism and who also tried to help their parents become less frightened and more accepting.

One thing that the authors would like to stress is that coming out is a painful process for most lesbians and gay men. The fear of anticipated rejection is an extraordinarily distressing experience. One of the most confusing aspects of the coming-out process is that of not knowing in advance when one is going to meet with negative responses. Here it is of utmost importance for the gay man or lesbian to be in touch with his/her own homophobia, because it is often extremely difficult to differentiate between personal projections and what is real.

Very often, the anxiety that is experienced when one is anticipating coming out is so great that one believes those he/she is coming out to will react in accordance to his/her own worst fears. For example, a person may be convinced that coming out will cause his/her parents to die, have a heart attack and/or maybe even disown him/her. This person may also be afraid that coming out will result in rejection by friends, derogatory remarks and ostracization by acquaintances, the loss of a job by an employer, and so forth. Upon further and very careful consideration, one may discover that these fears really did not belong to the other people after all—that, in fact, they belonged to the person who was thinking them.

To help differentiate between what possible reactions do and do not belong to those one is coming out to, it can be helpful to ask oneself such questions as the following: How strong is the relationship that exists between you and the other person? How open is the other person to differences? How well has your relationship weathered difficult times? Can the other person keep a secret if you so wish?

The coming-out process is affected by many factors. One's age is an important dimension. Coming out is different for an adolescent, a person in their early twenties, someone middle-aged, or a senior citizen. The developmental tasks for each of these ages have specific objectives to achieve, and the issues presented by homosexuality interface differently with each.

In her book *Growing Older, Getting Better: A Handbook for Women in the Second Half of Life,* Jane Porcino writes, "For some women, sexual orientation toward other women is established early in life. They have for years shared intimacy, companionship, love, and sex with other women, and they continue to do so in their later years. For others, identification or expression of bisexuality or lesbianism is delayed by cultural attitudes until later in life. Elaine, a forty-three-year-old woman, talks to the author about her own experience:

> I always suspected I was gay and spent many years trying to suppress those feelings and thoughts. Growing older gave me me. At last I'm able to do what I believe right for me. Oh yes, society still said no loud and clear, but now I discovered that I am not alone, not the only one—if only society would listen! My life with my lover is the happiest, strongest love I know—just two beautiful people loving, living, growing, and sharing together.[2]

Religion is another important factor. It can affect the degree to which one hates oneself. Most typically it defines how truly unacceptable, bad, or even evil a person can be by being gay or lesbian. Gender is an additional component. Lesbianism, while generally more tolerated than male homosexuality, is still seen as a threat in our society, and evokes many negative feelings and reactions. Just as female sexuality in general has a long history of being denied, so the expression of lesbian sexuality has specifically been denied. When recognized, it has frequently been admitted only in terms of masculine appearance or other stereotypes. Lesbians have to cope not only with the multitude of ambivalent cultural pressures all women are experiencing today, but also with their devalued status because they differ from their heterosexual counterpart in their choice of a life mate.

The following reminiscences by Marge McDonald from 1955 in the *Lesbian History Archives Newsletter* #10, Feb. 1988, p. 3, reflect some of the experiences one has to deal with when people act as if you do not exist.

> THE WAY WE WERE: Marge McDonald Diary Entry Describes Her First Visit to a Lesbian Bar—Columbus, Ohio—3/31/55. . . . Here are the Lesbian 50's in a mid-west bar—the tremendous courage and need that created them, the strategies created to find them, the codes of dress and behavior that protected a community from police entrapment—and most of all here is where Marge came home. 3/31/55. . . . After a while I brought up the subject of the queer bar and asked Sue where it was, being careful to mention that I wanted to go there with Ted. She showed me where it was. I was numb inside with anticipation, fear, excitement—everything.

Bev, the girl sitting beside me said she thought it might be fun to see such a place. . . . I was hoping she would, because for some crazy reason I didn't want to go in there by myself. I guess, I needed someone to bolster my courage. As we walked in the door, I was so excited I could hardly walk. . . .

Bev and I sat down in a booth. . . . After a while Bev said, "Let's go, I don't like this place very well." I replied, "Oh, I don't know, I sort of like it here." But we left and went down to Caseys, another bar and had a beer. I feigned sickness and got rid of her. 10:00 found me driving around the block near the Town Grill, trying to summon enough nerve to go in by myself.

Finally, having whipped up my courage, I walked in and took a seat among the girls at the bar. I was a wreck. My elbows were shaking even tho I had them propped on the bar. I was too frightened to look at anybody. . . . I had sat there what seemed like an hour but probably wasn't, when a pretty blonde walked up to me and said in a warm friendly voice, "I hope you don't think I'm being fresh but I have noticed that you are new here and that no one has been talking to you. They think you are a police woman. I'm Toni and I want you to feel free to walk up and say 'Hi' to me any time you see me."

. . . . I was so glad that Toni had spoken to me. I sat there looking first at one sign and then another and stealing glances at a boyish-looking girl behind the bar in slacks and a man's shirt.[3]

Although men have society's permission to be sexual and in fact are encouraged to do so, same sex behavior between males tends to receive more scorn than same sex behavior among females. In part this is due to the assumption that one of the men plays a female role in the relationship, which in society's eyes lowers his value as a "male" man. This tendency to be scornful can also be related to such factors as one's own insecurity about his sexuality and one's tendency to see females, and anything that appears to be effeminate, as inferior since "macho" still continues to be the name of the game for most people.

Actually men really grow up in a difficult situation. How many men does the reader know who have been encouraged in their growing-up years to tune into and express feelings other than joy, rage, and pride? In other words, how many men does the reader know who have been encouraged to tune into feelings of fear, pain, compassion, tenderness, etc.? How many men does the reader know who will openly cry? In our view, this is evidence of the oppression of men. Men can slap each other on the ass and hug and kiss each other, but only on the sports field where they are not expected to be sexual with one another. The emotional and physical closeness and spontaneity of gay men in all contexts definitely threatens the status quo.

Just as men are encouraged to be assertive and strong and silent, women are expected to be passive, ineffectual, emotional, fearful, dependent, chatty, etc. Women are supposed to marry and have children in order to be seen as successful in our society. If they have a profession it is expected to be secondary to their gender-related role as wife and/or mother. Lesbians do not fit this stereotype. By their very existence they challenge the status quo.

How does a counselor fit in to the process of coming out? How can you know if someone is truly heterosexual, homosexual, or bisexual? Are there signs? What makes one heterosexual?

Is there a heterosexual look? How do they dress? What about the jewelry they wear? Do straight men wear necklaces, rings, bracelets, and earrings? Do straight men wear earrings in a particular ear—the right ear or the left? Do straight women wear pants? Boots? What about ties? How do they talk?

If men gesture with their hands, can they be straight? Do they have a special language? Do they admire themselves in the mirror? Do they care about what they look like? Do straight men get manicures?

Do straight women only wear high heels? Do straight women always wear makeup and get permanents? Do they always wear a bra? What about shaving their legs or their underarms?

Can any of these questions be answered with definite yeses or noes? Many straight, gay, and bisexual people appear to have a lot in common. Many sweeping fashion trends among heterosexuals have been started by gay men and lesbians.

Nevertheless, is there a specifically homosexual look? Are there manners of dress, or behavior that is reserved exclusively for homosexuals? Can one truly be certain? These external signals are at best unclear.

For a heterosexual who is forced to rely on external signs to decide if someone else is gay, the consequences of making a mistake are relatively minor. For a person who has come to a first tentative belief that he/she is gay, the stakes are much higher. How can he/she find somebody else with the same inclination?

One certainly cannot just walk up to someone else and ask, "Are you gay?" So when a client talks to you about the pain connected with his/her isolation, how can you help?

Just as there are no definite signs to tell the client who else is gay, so there are no definite signs to tell the counselor if the client is truly homosexual either. But, does the counselor have to know? Why? What is wrong with simply joining the client in a mutual process of exploration? After all—one of the most basic principles in the helping services pertains to starting where your client is. If you have a preconceived idea that will interfere with your ability to be sensitive to your client, you will be working from your own agenda rather than that of your client.

How does one differentiate between a friend/client who is truly homosexual and one who is simply going through a temporary phase of sexual questioning? Initially you cannot, and you do not have to. But you can be certain that the person's struggle is real and to be taken seriously. During the course of this struggle, the friend/counselor must be careful not to become impatient. The process of self-discovery unfolds slowly. And the process can be very confusing, since the final outcome may not be predictable from the various stages traveled through. Sometimes individuals can be absolutely certain they are lesbian or gay from the very beginning of their quest. They get involved in same-sex relationships; they "come out" to family and friends as homosexuals; and later they discover that they are in fact heterosexual or bisexual.

So, how can one best explore sexual orientation issues with one's clients? Would you feel comfortable asking them if they were lesbian or gay? Is there a way to feel more comfortable? How do you know when such a question is appropriate? Is it something you initiate out of the blue or do you look for clues?

In trying to clarify our thinking about this dilemma let us focus our attention on what might happen in an interview with Gail, our young printer, who is concerned about her drinking. Gail had been worried that her counselor would find out she was a lesbian and react by not accepting her. This fear was a source of internal conflict for Gail, because she knew that if she was to get real help from her counseling she would have to risk revealing her lesbianism, and yet she deeply feared a negative response from her counselor to such a disclosure. In her ambivalence, Gail initially tried to get the feel of the waters:

Gail talked about having lots of women friends, while looking closely at the counselor's face for reactions. The counselor responded to the opening:

c. Are you married?
g. No, but I have had several relationships.
c. Do you think you have a problem forming or keeping relationships?
g. Yes, I tend to get into fights.
c. What triggers them off.
g. They usually take place when I'm drinking.
c. Tell me about your drinking.
g. I go to the bar where most of my friends are.
c. How often do you go?
g. Mostly every night.
c. How come?
g. That's where my friends are, and I do not like to drink alone.
c. What happens at the bar?
g. I dance, talk, and cruise.
c. Cruise?
g. Yeah, you know—see who I'm attracted to. See if they are looking at me.
c. What kind of people are you attracted to?
g. Good-looking, tall, dark, sexy, and fun.
c. *(Nods, smiles, and shows concern)* Do you have to drink to enjoy yourself?

Please look at the proceeding dialogue and see if you notice anything. What stands out the most? Let us change the dialogue:

c. Are you married?
g. No, but I've had several relationships.
c. With men or with women?
g. *(With relief and some trepidation)* Women.
c. How long have they lasted, etc.

Many counselors might not be comfortable asking a gender question this early in the interview, and much depends on sub-

jective impressions during the counseling session. Another way
the issue of sexual orientation could be raised, if the counselor is
familiar with the term *cruising* which many lesbians and gay men
use, is as follows:

C. What happens at the bar?
G. I dance, talk, and cruise.
C. Cruise—what does that mean?
G. You know—see who I'm attracted to, see if they are attracted
to me.
C. Do you cruise men or women?

The counselor has opened an avenue for Gail to "come out." If
Gail chooses not to respond to the invitation, it signifies that she
is not yet ready. It is too soon and too scary. She needs more time
to become acquainted and develop a sense of trust. It is important that the counselor note the evasion or denial and not push
the issue, but seek to return to the question of sexual orientation
at a later time when it seems more appropriate. If she were
heterosexual, Gail would most typically have made a clear statement that it was men she was cruising. Any ambiguity however
would be an indication that she very well may be lesbian.

As you can see from this example, one can ask very simple and
direct questions regarding sexual orientation interests without
implying a judgment. Yet the counselor may know that he/she is
asking a simple direct question and the client may still respond
by being offended. Since the counselor knows that the question
had simply been asked for a factual response with no judgments
attached—he/she can now explore the extent of the client's de-
fensiveness.

G. I've had several relationships.
C. With men or women?
G. Men or women—how could you ask me a question like that?
C. What's wrong with the question?
G. Do you think I'm gay?
C. I don't know—do you?
G. (*After a long pause*) Yes, but how did you know?
C. I didn't—that's why I asked you the question. But what I don't
understand is, why it upset you so much?
G. Oh, I'm not out to many people and I was afraid.

c. Keeping that secret must be very hard for you.

g. Yes—but I feel relieved that you know now.

c. I'm glad I know too because now the secret won't cause an obstacle in our work together.

Some counselors might have been tempted, out of discomfort, or curiosity, or bias, to pursue lesbianism as a problem in itself. If that is done the counselor has lost sight of the fact that Gail came because she has a drinking problem and not because she has a problem with being a lesbian.

What about situations where the therapeutic issue is the question of homosexuality? Let us say that a male client comes to you expressing great concern over his fear that he may be gay. He is afraid that his life will be ruined. He is sure from everything he has heard in his family while growing up that he would be disowned by them if he were gay. From all of the fag jokes he has heard among his peers, he fears that they, too, would reject him. He believes he has no alternative but to commit suicide if in fact he really is gay.

You, the counselor or friend, are listening to what this young man has to say. A lot of pressure is being placed on you. Maybe you would like to get up and run out of the room. Since you cannot do that what can you do? You may feel a lot of pressure to help this young man be straight. After all, he has expressed a suicide thought.

Here you are faced with many questions for yourself—some of which include: (1) Do you think that you have the power to make a person either straight or gay with your counseling advice? (2) Do you agree that suicide is a valid option for homosexuals—or for anyone, for that matter? (3) Do you think you would feel or even be responsible if he made a suicide attempt? (4) What problem do you focus on—suicide or sexual orientation? (5) Do you think that it is possible for one to decide on one's sexual orientation in a single counseling session or rap session with a friend?

First you will want to talk to the person and find out why he has these concerns about his sexual orientation and if he has had any actual same-sex experience. As you do this it is important that you emphasize that these answers need not be determinative after one single talk or interview. This is true in discussing any sexual matter. It is something you and he will need to explore over a period of time, so that you both can better understand what is going on. You will also need to listen to his fears in an empathetic manner, emphasizing that you understand that the discussion is terrifying for him. You will want to explore the various thoughts he has had about suicide. How will he do it? Has he ever tried? Does he think he really will try, and so on.

At this point you may find it necessary to tell the client that you cannot promise that he will discover himself to be heterosexual, homosexual, or bisexual, but that you can assure him you will do everything possible to help him understand what is happening to him. You may also find it advisable at this time to have him promise not to do anything self-destructive while he is going through the exploration process with you.

CL. I have to know right now—I can't stand the pressure. It feels like it's going to kill me if I don't know.

C. Tell me how it is killing you.

CL. Because if I'm gay, then nobody will like me—everyone will hate me.

C. How do you know?

CL. Because I've heard everything negative.

C. It is true that homosexuality is looked down on by a lot of people. Just as it is true that many other people believe "Gay is good." It's also true that this is a very serious and important issue for you. One that is too important and complex for us to handle or be able to resolve today.

CL. But what am I going to do?

C. One thing you can decide to do is only to talk to people you trust until we understand this further. Another thing which would be helpful is to read books on the subject. Is there anyone whom you trust?

CL. Yes—my younger sister.

C. How would you feel about discussing it with her?

CL. Well, maybe,—I don't think she'd talk to others if I asked her not to.

C. Now, about your thoughts of suicide—tell me about them. What are they?

CL. Last night after I went to a gay bar I thought of throwing myself in front of a car.

c. Have you ever had thoughts like that before?

CL. A few times. . . .

c. Have you ever tried to do anything?

CL. No, I couldn't bring myself to hurt myself.

c. So what you are saying is an example of how terrifying it is for you to think of yourself as being gay.

CL. Yeah.

c. I can appreciate your terror. Actually I anticipate that you will experience more terror as we continue to explore the question of your sexual orientation. Therefore I want to ask you—even though it may seen unnecessary—to promise me that you will not do anything to harm yourself while we are going through this process of exploration.

CL. *(With some relief)* OK.

c. One other thing—I want to be sure that you will contact me any time you are thinking of hurting yourself. I want to be there for you as much as I can. It's important for you to know that you are not alone in this.

There is no guarantee that a client will not commit suicide. All statements about suicide should be taken seriously. But they should also be heard as expressions of overwhelming pain and definite cries for help.

Since these are cries for help, it is important to indicate your concern and involvement, without becoming panicked and without being judgmental. It is very helpful to pay attention to thoughts of death as an expression of one's fear and self-hate, since further along if this person is thinking about coming out to his family he may express the same fear in very similar terms, e.g., "the news will kill my parents."

In this chapter we have attempted to look at various aspects of the "coming-out" process. We have yet to explore in depth the differing ethical, moral, and religious issues that relate not only to "coming out" but to homosexuality in general. These will be addressed in the following chapter.

4
Religion

All of us grow up with a sense of ethics, values, and morality, which we learn from our parental figures, religious institutions, schools, communities, and society at large. As little children we tend to accept what our parental figures tell us is "right" or "wrong." Often we may find that what we are taught at home and in our religious education is different from what we may experience in school, in our friends' homes, or through the media of television, movies, magazines, or what we come to by ourselves. Although we may question these differences, we ultimately tend to accept the teachings of our primary authority figures.

What we learn are standards of conduct and moral judgments regarding the rightness or wrongness of our own behavior and that of others. These standards or beliefs make up a specific system (ethics) that tend to become an integral part of us by the time we reach adulthood.

Often we are not even aware of their presence until we are confronted with an issue or situation that brings them into consciousness. Thus, if you are attracted to a member of the same sex, you may feel that there is something ethically or morally wrong with you because you are "not supposed" to be attracted to someone who is of the same gender.

What we learn is not necessarily something that has been overtly taught. Many times what we learn comes from attitudes, double messages, jokes, derisive remarks, etc. We frequently learn this at the same time we are being taught in school that all people are created equal. Clearly, there are double standards in our society.

One of these double standards has to do with the area of

sexual orientation. How often was homosexuality referred to in your family as a valid or viable life-style? Most of us have been expected by our parents to develop relationships with members of the opposite sex. Can you imagine your parents encouraging you to have a relationship with a member of the same sex? The possibility of our becoming involved in same-sex relationships is something that others "know" we would just never do. Even if our parents were to accept same-sex behavior for our peers, public figures, or for that matter their friends, the message may still be clear that this is not an acceptable alternative for us.

One reason that this might be so has to do with the fact that a large number of people believe that homosexual behavior is sinful or evil. Same-sex relationships are seen by many as a violation of the most basic codes of morality that occur in our society. These codes are frequently expressed in the writings of our Judeo-Christian religious tradition. For example:

In the Old Testament, Genesis 19:4–11, the story of Sodom and Gomorrah is often seen as referring to homosexual acts: the citizens of Sodom appear at Lot's door and want the visitors (two angels sent by God) to come out so that they might "know them." Lot desists and even offers to send out his daughters; the people refuse to leave and only do so when the angels strike them blind.[1]

The most common interpretation of this story has been that the people of Sodom were demanding an opportunity to commit homosexual acts with the angels of God who were Lot's guests. Supposedly—as the story goes—God destroyed Sodom because he was angry at the citizens for their immoral behavior. A further substantiation of this belief is noted in the fact that anal intercourse subsequently became known as sodomy and homosexual males have often been referred to as sodomites. Interestingly, although many heterosexual people also perform anal intercourse, one seldom hears them referred to as sodomites.

A different interpretation of the destruction of Sodom and Gomorrah appears in Ezekiel 16:49–50: "Behold, this was the iniquity of thy sister Sodom, pridefulness of bread, and abundance of idleness was in her and in her daughters, neither did she strengthen the hand of the poor and needy. And they were haughty, and committed abomination before me: therefore I took them away as I saw good."[2] This view of the Ezekiel story seems to indicate that God probably destroyed the city for its lack of hospitality, rather than for any homosexual thoughts or acts.

References to supposed homosexual conduct in the New Testament are even fewer than in the Old Testament. Current interpretations of Jesus' public statements do not indicate any such references. The New Testament references to homosexuality were written by Paul. For example, Romans I:26–27: "For this cause God gave them up unto vile affections: for even their women did change the natural use into that which is against nature: and likewise also the men, leaving the natural use of women, burned in their lust one toward another: men with men working that which is unseemly, and receiving in themselves that recompense of their error which was met."[3] It is interesting to note in the above verses that Paul recognized the existence of lesbian behavior, which is not noted at all in the Old Testament.

In Timothy I:10 we read, "for whoremongers, for them that defile themselves with mankind."[4] Are the writings about true homosexuals or about perversion? Father John McNeil, a Catholic scholar, suggests that there is ample evidence that the authors of the Bible thought of perversion as the committing of homosexual acts by those who were inclined by nature to be heterosexual.[5] Scanzoni and Mollenblatt, in their book *Is the Homosexual My Neighbor?* conclude that the New Testament has nothing to say in reference to the genuine condition of homosexuality, where intimate and long-lasting relationships between members of the same sex are established.[6] It is conceivable that lesbians and gay men as we know them today were just not known to the writers of the Bible.

Paul's words were to men who "gave up natural relations with women" yet gay men have no natural relationship with women to renounce. Their natural relationship is with men. The same would be true for lesbians. Their natural relationship is with women.

There is much within the Bible to inspire and guide us. It is a magnificent history book about the development of a people in a significant period of our civilizing process. However it is important to examine the theological context of its teachings in order to be clear about what it actually says, as opposed to what various people say it says, to us.

Many such people fail to address the issue of "love" that is central to Jesus' teachings. Christ deplored lust and the abuse of another person. He preached respectful and stable loving relationships. Lesbians and gay men desire these relationships as much as heterosexuals do. In Romans 14:14 we find, "I know and am persuaded by the Lord Jesus, that there is nothing unclean of itself: but to him that esteemeth any thing to be unclean of itself, to him it is unclean."[7]

When we read any religious writing, or any writing for that matter, it is imperative to think about who the writer is, whom they are writing for, where they come from, and what message it is that they are trying to get across.

For example, in this present book, the authors come from the Midwest and East Coast. One is Protestant by birth and the other was born a Catholic and converted to Judaism. Both are lesbians who are very definitely trying to help the reader gain a fuller understanding of what it is like for a person to be a homosexual with the intention of helping the reader become more compassionate towards and accepting of homosexuals. This clearly is not an unbiased book, yet it does present negative as well as positive images of lesbians and gay men as a way to help readers gain as complete a picture as possible from which to form their own opinion. An opinion that we hope will be sympathetic. Inclusion of some negative views can also help the reader gain further understanding of some of the difficulties homosexuals have to cope with while trying to formulate or re-form their own sense of identity.

As noted above, the authors do not think that all the biblical information is given "equal time," nor are possible other interpretations of the passages even opened up for discussion. For example, Ezekiel is not usually cited when the story of Sodom is used to make a case for the sinfulness of homosexuality.

Time and space do not permit us to explore in depth the Judeo-Christian influences and attitudes about homosexuality or explore those of other religions. As in earlier chapters, our primary goal is to highlight or spotlight how particular teachings or attitudes appear in our society and how they affect all of us— regardless of whether we are homosexual or heterosexual.

The authors have attempted to give some perspective on how religious teachings influence us by giving a few examples of selected biblical verses. We do not claim to be biblical scholars and we suggest that those interested in pursuing further the mystery of the Bible's teachings about homosexuality refer to the bibliography at the end of this book for suggested readings.

Our major point is that people who think they and/or their behavior are an abomination cannot love themselves, and in fact are often full of self-hate. This can present a problem for everyone.

The following two examples will illustrate what we mean.

Bobbie Griffith, the third child in a fundamentalist Christian family, kept diaries of his struggles as a gay young man. Many of his diaries contained his thoughts of being different and his fears of being punished by God.

"Why did you do this to me, God? Am I going to go to Hell? That's the gnawing question that is always drilling little holes in the back of my mind. Please don't send me to Hell. I'm really not that bad, am I? I want to be good. I want to amount to something. I need your seal of approval. If I had that I would be happy. Life is so cruel and unfair."

Bobbie committed suicide on August 27, 1983.[8]

Unlike Bobbie, Renata felt differently. On the "Geraldo Rivera Show" of March 3, 1989, which focused on "Lesbian Teens and Their Mothers," Renata responded to an audience question, "Does theology or the biblical context play some kind of role in the course that the ladies have taken?" by saying, "Yeah, I'd like to answer this question. I've been told by a fair number of people that I will burn in Hell because of the fact that I am a lesbian and proud of it. To which I respond that I will not—I refuse to believe in a God that will damn someone to Hell for loving someone else. I mean, I do not believe that any god would damn someone to Hell for loving someone else."[9]

Each person, whether religious or not, needs to figure out what he/she believes about homosexuality. Some people may turn to professionals and some may turn to friends or family members to help them in their search for answers. In the end it is the individual who must come to terms with what he or she really believes. Nobody can tell another person what to believe about homosexuality and expect it to be accepted at face value even though we all know people who try. Each one of us has to

go on his or her own search. In this endeavor pastoral counselors can be especially helpful with their more thorough knowledge of their religious teachings if they are open to alternative
life-styles.

This can also place a great burden on a counselor or a friend
with strong religious beliefs. Just as the authors want people to
become more accepting of lesbians and gay men, those with
strong religious beliefs may be inclined to persuade others to
adopt their particular orientations without allowing leeway for
the presentation of differing points of view or for the questioning of their own point of view. This tends to happen since many
people are convinced that homosexuality is sinful and because
they are not really interested in scholarly discussion about scrip-
tural fine points.

Religious bias may lead a friend, family member, or counselor
to be blind to the anguish of the person who is on his/her search
for understanding. This search is extremely important because it
involves a deep-seated conflict that many people never fully
resolve. It involves a great deal of self-loathing, recriminations,
and self-hate that can result in isolation, sexual acting out (both
heterosexual and homosexual), alcohol or drug abuse, and possible suicidal thoughts or behavior, etc.

> Mary Griffith used to hold fundamentalist Christian beliefs. She
> used to believe homosexuality was a sin. She used to believe that if
> (her son) Bobby prayed hard enough, he would become straight.
> But Bobby found that praying didn't change a thing. And so,
> like so many young gays and lesbians who struggle to accept
> themselves, he decided that death was his only escape from the
> pain of being different.
> Bobby's death changed Mary's world. She stopped attending
> Walnut Creek Presbyterian Church. She is now a firm supporter of
> the gay movement."[10]

It is not unusual for lesbians and gay men, in their efforts at
dealing with these issues, to cite the Bible frequently as validation for their very painful conviction that they are bad or evil.
How would you respond if a friend or client asked you if you
believed what the Bible says about homosexuality? Would you
even know what the Bible says? Would you know that there are

different interpretations about what the Bible says? Would you be able to discuss the whole issue of whether or not the Bible says anything at all about homosexuality as we know it today?

The following are some examples of how any of us might respond to situations or questions involving a person's fear and/ or conviction that he/she is bad, sinful, or evil, and will be punished because he/she may be lesbian or gay. A young man is discussing someone he met at a bar whom he liked.

c. Are you going to see him again?

CAL. Well, I don't know.

c. What don't you know?

CAL. I don't know if I'm ready to go out with someone yet.

c. How come?

CAL. It doesn't feel right.

c. What doesn't feel right?

CAL. I'm afraid I could really like him a lot.

c. What's wrong with that?

CAL. Then it would be real.

c. What would be real?

CAL. I guess my being gay. One-night stands have not felt like I was gay, more like just exploring.

c. Is there something wrong with being gay?

CAL. Well, of course there is—everyone knows that.

c. I don't, tell me.

CAL. You've got to be kidding.

c. No. I'm serious. I'd like to hear what you think is wrong.

CAL. Don't you know that the Bible says that homosexuality is a sin?

c. No, not as I understand it. How do you understand it?

CAL. They always said in church that it was bad. It isn't natural. You are supposed to get married and have children.

c. Is it written any place that homosexuality is bad?

CAL. Actually I'm not sure.

c. If you are not sure how come you're so positive that homosexuality is bad?

CAL. I guess I never really thought about it or questioned it before. I just assumed it was true.

This line of questioning can encourage your client to think about whether or not what he or she has assumed to be a truth is really true for him/her. Many of us give little thought to what we have been taught in our formative years. It is only when we find ourselves forced to examine our beliefs that we begin to become aware of which are basic truths, which are learned values and rules, and which are valid subjects for reappraisal.

Another example of an acceptance of negative values about homosexuality might be seen in the following:

C. How did you learn that homosexuals are bad?

DON. I remember that even as a kid my father told me to stay away from queers, especially in gym class.

C. Did you know what he meant by queer?

DON. I wasn't really sure—he never told me exactly what a queer was. I guessed it meant someone who looked and acted different or strange.

C. Why would that make them bad?

DON. That's what I couldn't figure out, so I asked my friend what a queer was and he told me it was a fag. Another friend told me that a fag was a homosexual.

C. What did that teach you about homosexuality?

DON. Actually, now that I'm talking about it with you, it didn't teach me anything at all about homosexuals. But it sure did teach me a lot about people's homophobia, mine included.

C. And what was that?

DON. I guess it was the faces they made and their tone of voice. They seemed to look down on gays and made fun of them, so I thought there was something wrong with them. Wrong enough, so that I knew I wouldn't want to be one of them.

As you can see from this example, the authors are not saying you have to change people's attitudes. However, we do realize the importance of looking at attitudes and questioning whether they reflect present-day thoughts and values. A lot of times we were taught things like, "Eat your carrots, they're good for your eyes." So we ate our carrots and figured we would always have good vision and never have to wear glasses. It was rarely ever a question of whether we liked the taste of carrots or not. It was more a matter of our doing what we were told to do. Both of these authors have to wear glasses—but we ate our carrots like good little girls.

We all have been raised to believe that certain things are good for us and certain things are bad for us. As children and young people, many of us learned not to question our elders. Unfortunately this can create problems for us as adults. As children we tried to be "good," but what do we do as adults when we find we do not necessarily agree with what we were taught? What do we do when we find the things we were taught do not bring the promised results, e.g., carrots and good vision? What do we do when the things we have been taught make us feel guilty?

Guilt and the fear of rejection are depicted in the following dialogue with a thirty-year-old lesbian who wishes to become pregnant:

C. I haven't heard you say anything about your parents.

MARSHA. Well, that's the one thing I'm concerned about.

C. What's that?

MARSHA. Uh! Well, ugh! My parents.

C. What about your parents? Have you told them?

MARSHA. No, I'm afraid to.

C. Oh! Perhaps we should talk about it.

MARSHA. Well, you see they are very religious people who believe in marriage and the family and, well, I haven't even told them I'm a lesbian yet.

C. How come?

MARSHA. When I was growing up, I was taught very clearly that homosexuals are perverted and unnatural. Can you think of anything more unnatural in their eyes than a pervert wanting to have a baby? It would be truly unacceptable. I'm sure that they would disown me. They are already upset that I'm thirty years old and not married.

C. Why is that upsetting to them?

MARSHA. 'Cause they want grandchildren. They think grandchildren are the "reward" you get for raising your own children "right."

C. Don't you think they'd like and love your child?

MARSHA. Not if they knew I was a lesbian. Not if I didn't have a husband.

C. Do you think that there's something wrong with that?

MARSHA. Yeah, I guess so. The baby wouldn't have a father in the traditional sense and I guess I also believe that you're supposed to be married if you have a child. Anyway, that's what I've been taught. I guess it does make me feel kinda guilty. Like I'm doing something wrong, yet there doesn't seem to be anything wrong in my mind when I think about becoming a single parent. Anyway, that is what I've been taught and I can't sort it all out, so sometimes I try not to think about it at all.

It is important for all of us to realize that these so-called painful topics are not necessarily so painful that they should be avoided. Given the opportunity, most people tend to be very willing, almost gratefully so, to enter into a discussion, especially when they feel that the expressed interest and concern are sincere. It is through the process of talking that we are able to see what our thoughts really sound like, to hear the contradictions, to hear some things we don't like, to hear some things that please us, etc.

The authors believe that you cannot help a person deal with the "whole" issue of homosexuality unless you explore a person's spiritual and/or religious thoughts, feelings, and attitudes. Although this may be painful or uncomfortable for both participants it is more than worth it in the long run.

It also may be helpful if you have an idea of where different denominations stand on homosexuality. The following chart may be helpful to you. It reflects the results of a poll conducted by the *San Francisco Examiner* in 1989:[11]

Gays and Religion

	Let open gays join	Ordain open gays	Consider homosexuality a sin	Have a formal teaching policy on homosexuality
United Methodist	Yes	No	"Not officially"	National Reconciling Congregation Program involves training, etc.; may decide on supporting gays at all levels, including ordination
Mormon	No	No	Yes	Chastity and fidelity policy
Roman Catholic	Yes	Only if celibate	If practiced	Yes; traditional policy of any sexual activity outside marriage being wrong
Baptist	Yes	No	Viewed same as other sins	American Baptists and Southern Baptists differ and churches are autonomous; one may be open to gays and another not

Gays and Religion *(continued)*

	Let open gays join	Ordain open gays	Consider homosexuality a sin	Have a formal teaching policy on homosexuality
United Church of Christ	Yes	Yes	No	Encourages gays and lesbians to join; sexual orientation not a barrier to ordination
Episcopal	Yes	No	No	Urging congregations to provide dialogues on human sexuality
Lutheran	Yes	No*	Yes	Not in God's original plan
Presbyterian	Yes	No	Views differ	No, except for not ordaining gays
Moslem	No	No	Yes (one of worst)	"A homosexual would be encouraged to change"
Buddhist	Yes	Yes	No	No
Reform Judaism	Yes	No**	No	Since 1987, supports inclusion of gay Jews

*One branch considering   **Under consideration

EXAMINER GRAPHICS

You as a counselor or friend cannot be expected to answer all the questions asked of you. You cannot expect yourself to, that is unfair. The most important thing you can do is to encourage the other person to explore his/her thoughts and feelings as fully as possible. In doing this it is, of course, of the utmost importance that you be aware of your own thoughts, feelings, and beliefs and try not to let them interfere or impinge on the other's process.

You may find that it would be helpful to refer your friend or client to a house of worship where you know lesbians and gay men are welcome. Some churches have reconsidered their thinking about homosexuality. The United Church of Christ has affirmed privacy as a right for adults in consenting sexual relationships. Other churches such as the Episcopal (which started a dialogue on sexuality) and the United Methodist (which began a major study of homosexuality) are seriously looking at their teachings and practices regarding homosexuality.

Despite this, the Methodists and Presbyterians still do not ordain active homosexuals. The Unitarian Universalists, the

United Church of Christ, and the Disciples of Christ do consider ordaining lesbians or gay men. Bishop Paul Moore, Jr., ordained Ellen Marie Barrett on January 10, 1977, as a minister of the Episcopal Church. Some bishops and clergy were upset by the ordination. In the book, *Take a Bishop Like Me,* Paul Moore, Jr., included a letter to his colleagues regarding the ordination— some parts of which are quoted below by permission:

Dear Brothers:
. . . 4. Persons known, or virtually known, to be homosexual have been ordained for years. The only difference between such persons, whom many of us have ordained, and Ellen Barret, is her candor. Candor, or, if you will, honesty is not a bar to ordination.
. . . Her ordination was not a political act and did not seek to make a statement about homosexual activity: it was, like any ordination, the solemn laying on of hands upon a person carefully and prayerfully chosen.
. . . In shifting away from an exclusively procreative view of sex to one of sex as a human expression of love, we move beyond explicit biblical guidance. I pray that the Holy Spirit will guide us. The Church has reawakened to the realization that Truth is an open-ended process of progressive revelation, and what we are witnessing in our time with regard to human sexuality is just such a process.
For most people, however, this rethinking of the morality of sexual expression is yet to be extended to homosexual persons. I believe that their recognition as full members of the Church with the opportunities, rights, and responsibilities of all other members is based ultimately on Jesus' view of human nature as reflected in the Gospel. Again and again, He broke through the prejudices of the day to accept and lift up those rejected and downgraded by others. And just as the reasons for their rejection were often beyond their control, so the homosexual person's condition is generally not a matter of conscious choice.
The forces that shape sexual orientation are still somewhat mysterious, but there is general agreement that our sexuality is forged at an incredibly early age, long before puberty. Thus, a person's sexual preference is not in the category of sin, and the sometimes violent social prejudice against the homosexual condition comes painfully close to the recorded targets of Jesus' preaching."[12]

More recently, in January 1990, the Lutheran Church ordained its first homosexual minister.
There are also gay and lesbian groups in the different de-

nominations to which to refer people. These include Dignity (Catholic), Integrity (Episcopal), Axios (Eastern and Orthodox Christians), United Universalists for Lesbian/Gay Concern, Lutherans Concerned, United Church of Christ Coalition for Lesbian and Gay Concerns, Seventh Day Adventist Kinship International, Presbyterians for Lesbian/Gay Concerns and the "More Light" program, Evangelicals Concerned, Inc., Gay People in Christian Science, and Friends for Lesbians and Gay Concerns. Also American Baptists Concerned, Brethren-Mennonite Gay Caucus, Moravians Concerned, Unitarian Office for Gay Concerns, and Affirmation (Gay Mormon Underground). Some United Methodists offer "Affirmation" congregations that welcome gays as well as AIDS ministries in large cities. In addition, local churches may have groups, and it is important to inform yourself whenever possible of these resources. There are also gay synagogues to be found in some of the larger cities, for example Congregation Sha'ar Zakov in San Francisco and Congregation Beth Simchat Torah in New York City. There is also the Metropolitan Community Church that was founded by the Reverend Troy Perry for gay men and lesbians, and which is open to all. Some of these churches can be found in predominantly Spanish-speaking neighborhoods as well.

Books may be helpful also. An increasing number of books that deal with the issue of religion and homosexuality have been written in the past decade. The titles of some of these books can be found in the reference section at the end of this book.

The reader still may not think that religion is important. Friends and clients may not bring up spiritual or religious issues directly because they know that it is not necessarily a popular topic to discuss. They may have been teased or put down in the past for having expressed concerns of a religious nature. This lack of initiative from a person might be interpreted as confirmation that religion is not important.

That is a mistake. All of us have been brought up with some kind of religious orientation—even if we consider ourselves atheists. It is very helpful and often enlightening to make a point of asking about one's religious beliefs and how they affect one's sexual orientation and behavior. For example, a person could go through a counseling experience without ever discussing his/her religious and spiritual beliefs. The counseling could have been experienced as having been successful. However, that person might find that he/she always has a sense of guilt, shame, or discomfort whenever the topic of God or a higher Being is raised in a conversation. This might be very different if the counselor or friend had only thought to explore religion and spirituality.

This exploration can be a very exciting process in personal growth. We are all homophobic to some extent, even those who consider themselves to be the most enlightened. The more we can accept this fact as a truth the more we will be open to new levels of consciousness in ourselves and others.

5

Lesbian and Gay Youth

It is taken for granted that the development of social and sexual identity is a critical task of preadolescence and adolescence. There are numerous books, both on a professional and nonprofessional level, which deal with childhood and teenage issues of growth and development. There has also been an increase in the publication of how-to books and fictional works for youth related to questions about dating and other aspects of social relationships. Unfortunately, much of the literature and mass-media coverage fails to address sexual orientation issues. The assumption is made, however, that all children will grow up to be heterosexual, rather than acknowledging that some children may be bisexual and some will be homosexual.

How often have you thought in terms of lesbian and gay youth? Thought of what their social and sexual questions might be? Thought of what their needs are, as distinct from needs of heterosexual youths? And if you did think about lesbian and gay youths, how many of you thought about them as "just going through a stage?" that they will outgrow or as having a problem that must be rectified immediately before it becomes too serious. The authors have found that many people have not thought specifically enough about what these young people may experience in their lives, even though they may wish to be supportive or even think of themselves as supportive and accepting.

Not many people are aware that most lesbian and gay youths have known about their feelings for members of their same sex from a very young age. Many do not "blame" their parents for their sexual orientation. Nor for that matter do the youths believe that they have been taught to be lesbian or gay by others who are older than them. They just know what their feelings are and that they are attracted socially, affectionally, and sexually to members of their own sex.

In the preface to his book *Reflections of a Rock Lobster,* Aaron Fricke writes,

This is a book about growing up gay. But before I get into the story, I want to briefly discuss the questions that so many people have asked me. The most common is: "Why are you gay?"

The popular belief is that homosexuality is caused by a domineering mother. My mother and father both gave me a great deal of love and attention; by no means was my mother emotionally domineering. And at 4 feet 7 inches my mother is certainly not physically domineering either.

Another theory is that a sexual assault by an older man leads boys to become homosexual. I was never sexually assaulted during my childhood. There was a time when I was seven and my sixteen-year-old baby sitter tried to make me touch her rear end—but I merely passed off the incident as straight whimsiness and made her give me ten dollars not to tell my parents. I don't see how this could have made me switch sexual preferences.

So I did not have a domineering mother, my parents loved me, and I was never sexually assaulted by an older person. Furthermore, my mother was not doing speed at the time of conception, I was never exposed to high level radiation, and I never read a Truman Capote book before age ten. Why, then, am I gay?

. . . People also ask, "What is it that you hate about yourself that made you a homosexual? What a ridiculous question! I never had a low self-esteem that would make me gay. At one point, though, the reverse happened. Being homosexual led me to have a low self-esteem when I first became aware of society's attitudes about homosexuality.[1]

Aaron's example is unusual. He was outspoken about how people reacted to his being a gay adolescent. Many young lesbians and gay youths are also concerned that they are different, but problems can arise for them because they are afraid to discuss their feelings with parents, peers, or other significant people in their lives, even though they may want to. Problems can also arise when lesbian or gay youths try to share their feelings with someone they are attracted to. Very often they are rebuffed, publicly made fun of, scorned, ostracized, or rejected in other ways—unless that person feels the same way, which may very well happen.

Some problems that can arise from negative interactions or fear of negative interactions may include poor self-acceptance, extreme sensitivity to being misunderstood, hurt, or rejected, poor school attendance or performance, social withdrawal, substance abuse, participation in prostitution or pornography (for both females and males), suicide ideation and attempts, and running away from or leaving home.

Part of the overall difficulty for these young people is reflected in the fact that they not only have very few role models to identify with, but they also have trouble finding, meeting, and relating to other young people similar to themselves. As Rachel (Rivera 1989) expressed it:

> I was thinking that I would never fit in with anyone else. I'd never be part of the crowd. I didn't want to be different from everyone else.[2]

Another part of the difficulty is connected to the high degree of conformity among adolescents to stereotypical gender role behavior. Boys are usually expected to be macho males with strong interests in sports, physical strength, and fitness, the out-of-doors, beer, and girls. Girls are expected to be "feminine," have a low tolerance for alcohol, and be preoccupied with how they look and with attracting males. There is some latitude for girls to participate in sports (she's just being a tomboy) but they are usually expected to outgrow these interests during puberty.

One of the phenomena that occurs in adolescence is the need to belong, to be accepted by one's peer group. "The majority of the guys my age are mirror images of the next: hands in pockets, similar dress (jeans, T-shirts, earth shoes) and always excessively nice to any available female."[3] In order to be accepted it is typically believed that it is necessary to be similar to everyone else. This leaves very little room for individual differences—which means that your "average" emerging lesbian or gay teenagers will not go out of their way to draw attention to themselves via any nonheterosexual questions or behavior. After all—if you do not hear other kids raising sexual orientation questions—who in his/her right mind is going to stick his/her neck out with questions? You know that you might be called a degrading name, such as "faggot" or "lezzie."

The concept of individuality or individual differences (although highly praised and prized) does not really exist in adolescence. You can only be individual within acceptable limits. It seems to be a contradiction—how can you be an individual and at the same time conform? How do adolescents know the limits of acceptability for differences? How do they figure out the differences?

In many ways adolescents appear very individualistic: they wear weird clothes, they speak a strange language, they do odd things with their hair, they become obsessed with particular musicians and music, and they are very impassioned with everything they believe to be true. But there are limits. You and I may not see them, which is interesting since we knew them when we were their age. All of the above behavior really just sets adolescents apart from adults. But one area where adolescents and adults are similar is in their assumption that everyone is and will be heterosexual.

All adolescents are limited by stereotypical sex role behavior, but lesbian and gay teenagers are even more limited. When any nonaccepted and unexpected behavior can bring a label of different or deviant, gay, or lesbian youth—who clearly are "deviant"—will be more secretive than anyone about their identity. These secrets can become burdensome, anxiety producing, and oppressive as seen in our earlier example of Luis.

Gay and lesbian adolescents also keep "secrets" from their parents and tend not to share important concerns with them. This occurs because the kids know that their parents have certain stereotypical expectations of them that they may not be able to meet. "I still live at home, which gets a little impossible at times because I haven't told my parents. They understand that I've always been more 'gentle' and have left it at that. If they were ever to ask if I were gay, I would say yes and explain it the best I could. I think it would hurt them terribly, but then I think of all the times I was hurt by trying to please them by going steady and dating. I tried to be 'normal,' even though it was against my feelings, but it just didn't work. I feel it would be better if my parents knew and understood, but at this point I wouldn't be the first to bring it up in conversation."[4]

In addition, a young boy may have difficulty expressing to his parents his interest in ballet, interior decorating, or any other profession that has been stereotyped and associated in our society with being a homosexual. A girl may be hesitant to express an interest in bodybuilding or fire fighting because those interests are viewed as too masculine.

Teenagers also know that their parents have a certain image of what they think their children will be like as they grow older. The parents often picture their children doing such things as going to college (maybe even their own college), becoming romantically involved and marrying someone of the opposite sex, providing their parents with grandchildren, buying their own home, having at least one car, and generally perpetuating the "American dream."

These expectations provide the parents with new sets of roles as in-laws and grandparents, roles that are very important since they will have lost their roles as primary caretakers of their offspring. It also provides them with a focus of attention both for themselves and in their interactions with others. For example, we all know the importance of wedding plans, the new life of the married child, the excitement around the anticipated grandchildren, and the pride parents feel as their children succeed and get ahead in their careers. Parents share this news with their peers and the news not only speaks of the children's successess but is experienced by many as also reflecting the parents' success in raising their children "well." All this can weigh heavily on adolescents who know that their needs and actions are going to disappoint their parents.

There are many signs that are important for an adolescent to consider before he/she decides to come out to parents or others. It will be helpful for us as counselors and friends to look at some of these considerations more closely.

Adolescents tend to be very concrete and in a rush. They also tend to think that each of their immediate thoughts and feelings is absolute and real. This can mean that if an adolescent experiences any feelings for a member of the same sex, he or she might begin to fear that he or she is lesbian or gay. Some of them might experience a need to decide immediately that this is true, because the anxiety that they are experiencing is so great. In all situations, but particularly in this kind, it is important to take these adolescents very seriously, while attempting to help them look at some of the possible implications of their "rush to the truth." They need to be helped to understand that it can take time and further exploration to find out whether they really are lesbian or gay, or if this is merely a phase in their emotional development. This can be an extremely delicate process, since talking about sexual issues at all between adolescents and adults is hard enough even before one considers the possible additional dimension of homosexuality or bisexuality.

Adolescent sexuality can be a difficult topic among adults, including even counselors. One reason is that adolescents are minors and we may fear that we might be held responsible for their subsequent behavior once we begin to explore questions of sexual orientation with them. This is particularly true if the teenager in question happens to turn out to be truly lesbian or gay. The anticipation of parental upset, legal issues, and agency pressures can be burdensome for a person who is working on these issues with an adolescent. Yet before adolescents decide to "come out" to their family and friends, it is important that they feel confident about their sexual orientation. Let us imagine a possible conversation with an eighteen-year-old who would like to discuss her attraction for other young women. Cary would like to come out to both her parents.

CARY. I've been thinking a lot about coming out to my parents but I do not know what to say to them.

C. Well, before we think about what you want to say let's think about how comfortable you are with your sexual orientation.

CARY. What do you mean?

C. Before you come out to someone, it's important that you feel sure of who you are and as comfortable as possible with yourself.

CARY. Why?

C. Because you can anticipate that the people you are telling will not feel comfortable. They'll probably be upset. They may get angry or hurt and try to talk you out of it.

CARY. So what?

C. If you feel comfortable you may not get as hurt or angry in return. You will be better able to listen and know when others are having a hard time. Maybe like you did when you first started to wonder about yourself.

CARY. Yeah, but my parents are grown-ups.

c. So-o?

CARY. Why wouldn't they understand?

c. Wait a minute, how do you think they'll respond?

CARY. Well, I think they'll be angry. My mother will cry . . .

c. And your father?

CARY. He'll be mad and walk out of the room without saying anything.

c. So, maybe we can look at how you might feel if in fact that's what happens.

CARY. It will probably be pretty earthshaking.

c. Do you think all that might make you doubt yourself?

CARY. Yeah well, but I guess I just want them to understand.

c. It will take them time, but the clearer that you are about yourself the less confusing it will be for all of you.

Equally important to discuss and decide upon is the whole issue of whom the adolescent wants to "come out" to—should it be mother, father, or both parents? How does one decide? Who does he/she feel most comfortable with? Who does he or she usually take his or her problems to? Who understands best? It has been the authors' experience that very often people tend to choose to "come out" to their mothers first, sometimes to both parents together, and least frequently to their fathers first.

Barbara is eighteen and would like to "come out," but she is not sure whom to do it with—her mom, dad, or both together.

BARBARA. It's really hard.

c. What is?

BARBARA. Trying to figure who to come out to.

c. Why?

BARBARA. This is serious. Once I start talking there is no going back.

c. Do you want to tell them together or individually?

BARBARA. I don't know, but one seems easier than two.

c. Why?

BARBARA. Well, there's only one of me.

c. Well, let's think about how you would do it, which one would you choose?

BARBARA. My mother.

c. How would you go about telling her?

BARBARA. I could tell her when we're cleaning up together after dinner.

c. How do you think she will react?

BARBARA. I don't know, sometimes I wonder if she already knows or suspects.

c. That's an interesting point. Very often parents do—but hearing the reality of it can still be upsetting.

BARBARA. I know. That's what I'm afraid of. I don't want to hurt her.

c. Who can your mother talk to?

BARBARA. I don't think that she'd talk to any of her friends. It's a small town. You really stand out if you are different.

c. How about your father?

BARBARA. I'm sure she'd talk to him about it.

c. How do you think he would feel about her being the one to tell him?

BARBARA. I think that he might feel hurt.

c. What would it be like of you told your mother and asked her not to tell your father until you shared it with him?

BARBARA. That would be hard, because she'd have no one to talk to—and he'd probably sense that something was bothering her. . . . Maybe it would be better if I told them both together."

In the preceding example, Barbara decided to tell both of her parents together. Very often it is the case that the person who is coming out decides to come out to just one parent because he or she knows that the other parent will be partially or totally rejecting. Sometimes that rejection can go as far as not wanting to see their child again. The person coming out loves that parent and would prefer living a double life, or one in the closet, to being disowned by one parent, which, if the child were thrown out of the house, could possibly lead to the loss of the other parent as well.

Another factor in coming out is timing—as seen in this vignette with Paul, a fifteen-year-old who has just told his counselor that he wants to tell his parents that he is gay.

PAUL. I think I'll tell them tonight.

c. Why tonight? This all seems very sudden.

PAUL. Because I'm sick and tired of their pressuring me to date girls.

C. I can appreciate your frustration, but let's think about this. It sounds like you want to get back at them.

PAUL. I do. You don't know what it's like—all they talk about is girls this and girls that. I feel like exploding. You'd think that girls are the only people in the world. I just want them to stop. Their pressure is making me hate girls.

C. Paul, I don't know what it's like to live in your house but I do know that when we do things in confusion and anger we often don't achieve what we set out to do. If you're feeling so desperate I wonder if tonight is a good time to come out to them.

PAUL. Why not?

C. Because it's a punishment. . . . You sound like you want to hurt them.

PAUL. So-o-o?

C. You have told me that your experience of yourself as a gay person is something very special to you. Ideally you would want to share that information with your parents because you love them and are feeling close to them—not because you are angry at them.

PAUL. So what can I do?

C. Don't confuse the issues. Talk to them about what's really upsetting you, which is their pushing you to date girls.

PAUL. How can I do that?

C. What do you think?

PAUL. I can't think. I'm too mad.

C. Explain how its making you feel like you want to hate girls, and you know you don't want that. Tell them you have to go at your own pace and even though you understand that they are concerned about you—the way that they are showing it isn't helpful to you.

PAUL. Well, you do have a point. If I can do that I may be able to get them off my back. I can tell them about being gay at another time when I'm not mad at them.

Everyone wants to be understood. In the case of homosexuality, it is important for the counselor or concerned friend to help the person who is contemplating "coming out" to realize that it is very difficult for most heterosexual people to understand how anyone could choose a person of the same sex as a love object. They too have been brought up to believe that homosexuality is bad, sick, deviant, sinful, and something to be ashamed of, etc.

However, it is reasonable to anticipate that after a period of time (which often can be a long period of time) those to whom a person is "coming out" can come to accept their homosexuality. The authors believe that it is of utmost importance for persons "coming out" to be helped to understand and anticipate the difficulties the person(s) they reveal themselves to may have in accepting the news. All they have to do is think about the difficulties that all groups who are different from one another have in understanding each other: e.g., blacks, Latinos, and whites; Christians, Jews, and Catholics; men and women; children and adults.

Some people who see understanding as the only goal in "coming out" may not value and/or realize the importance of acceptance. Yet being accepted can often be more important in the long run than being understood, because it is more within the realm of possibility. How often have you heard someone say, "I may not understand what you're doing, but I can accept it because it is important for you"? Understanding may come later.

The most important lesson is not to give up hope in life or yourselves. In her impassioned "Plea from a Mother," Mary Griffith, whose son Bobbie committed suicide at age twenty, writes,

> To all the Bobbies and Janes out there, I say these words to you, as I would to my own precious children:
> Please don't give up hope in life, or in yourselves. You are very special to me, and I am working very hard to help make this life a better and safer place for you to live in.
> I firmly believe—though I did not back then—that my son Bobby's suicide is the end result of homophobia and ignorance within most Protestant and Catholic churches, and consequently within society, our public schools, our own family.
> Bobby was not drunk, nor did he use drugs. It's just that we could never accept him for who he was—a gay person.
> We hoped God would heal him of being gay. According to God's word, as we were led to understand it, Bobby had to repent or God would damn him to hell and eternal punishment.
> Blindly, I accepted the idea that it is God's nature to torment and intimidate us.

That I ever accepted—*believed*—such depravity of God toward my son or any human being has caused me much remorse and shame.

What a travesty of God's love, for children to grow up believing themselves to be evil, with only a slight inclination toward goodness, and that they will remain undeserving of God's love from birth to death.

Looking back, I realize how depraved it was to instill false guilt in an innocent child's conscience, causing a distorted image of life, God and self, leaving little if any feeling of personal worth.

Had I viewed my son's life with a pure heart, I would have recognized him as a tender spirit in God's eyes.

I would have seen a life that, for the most part, parallels the heterosexual life—being, learning, working, loving and caring for another human being, having someone to grow old with, someone to share the joys and sorrows of life with, someone to share God's wonderful world with.

We never thought of a gay person as an equal, lovable, and valuable part of God's creation. What a travesty of God's unconditional love.

Is it any wonder our young people give up on love, as Bobby did, and the hope of ever receiving the validation they deserve as beautiful human beings?

Is it any wonder suicide statistics are increasing among young people, and even more so among gays and lesbians?

Bobby dropped out of Los Lomas High School in Walnut Creek in April 1981, two months before his graduation.

I believe if a gay counseling and education program like Project 10 had been available to him, he might be alive today.

With the right help to fight the homophobia surrounding him, he might have found the hope and encouragement he needed to finish school.

Walnut Creek's schools still don't have a Project 10, the program that helps gay teens in the Los Angeles schools.

But, as a result of my son's death, I have joined other caring people to try to make a pathway with knowledge and understanding within our public school system, a pathway that in time may be traveled with dignity and freedom from fear, for gay and lesbian students, and any student who is subjected to discrimination.

Promise me you will keep trying. As Tina Turner says in her song, "Love and compassion, their day is coming, all else are castles built in the air."

Bobby gave up on love. I hope you won't You are always in my thoughts.

With Love,
Mary Griffith[5]

There are some organizations available to lesbian and gay youths in the United States. Four of these include: The Hetrick-Martin Institute at 401 East West Street, New York City, New York, 10014 (212-633-8920); Sexual Minority Youth Assistance League, 1228 17th Street, NW, Washington, DC 20036 (202-296-0221); Horizons, 3225 North Sheffield Avenue, Chicago, Illinois, 60657 (312-472-6469); and The Gay and Lesbian Community Service Center, 1213 North Highland Avenue, Hollywood, California, 90038 (213-464-7400).

A final point the authors would like to make in this regard is that it is important for the friend/counselor to help the adolescent realize that his/her problems are separate from those of his/her parents. The parental concern for example of "what did I do wrong?" has nothing to do with the adolescent.

In the following Dear Abbey letter, which is similar to many written to columnists by confused and/or guilty parents and which appeared in a 1981 issue of the *San Francisco Chronicle,* "Puzzled in Hope" writes:

"Dear Abbey: I have a beautiful talented thirty-year-old daughter who is a lesbian, and I have always blamed myself for that. When she was a little girl, she hated dresses, so I let her wear blue jeans and T-shirts just like her brothers wore. I didn't think a thing of it at the time, but now I realize I helped to make a tomboy out of her. I blame myself for not insisting that she dress and act like a girl instead of putting her in boys' clothes and encouraging her to play boys' games with her brothers and their friends.

"So, my question is, if I didn't contribute to the way she turned out, how in the world did it happen?"[6]

We would like to point out that first of all the parents did not do anything wrong, and secondly, it is their problem, not their child's, if they think that they did something wrong in raising their child who happened to be a lesbian or gay male.

Abigail Van Buren clearly enunciated our point of view in her reply to "Puzzled":

> "Dear Puzzled: Don't blame yourself. Millions of little girls are tomboys and prefer jeans to dresses, yet the vast majority of them do not become lesbians. The causes of lesbianism, like those of male homosexuality, are complex and not fully understood as yet, but there is growing evidence that many lesbians are born with a predisposition in that direction.
>
> "The important thing to remember is that sexual preference is not a matter of choice: it is determined at a very early age. Children who grow up to be homosexuals need their parents' love and understanding no less than other children do. In fact, they need it more."[7]

In 1935 Sigmund Freud wrote an understanding "Letter to an American Mother" whose son was homosexual. In it he said, "Homosexuality is assuredly no advantage, but it is nothing to be ashamed of, no vice, no degradation, it cannot be classified as an illness. . . . Many highly respectable individuals of ancient and modern times have been homosexuals, several of the greatest men among them (Plato, Michelangelo, Leonardo da Vinci, etc.). It is a great injustice to persecute homosexuality as a crime, and a cruelty, too."[8]

In most situations parents will have concerns relating to themselves and their own adequacies as parents. Referral to a wonderful organization known as Parents and Friends of Lesbians and Gays (Parents FLAG) would be very helpful. Although Parents FLAG was officially formed in 1981, the initial inspiration for the group came from a fourth-grade teacher named Jeanne Manford, who in 1972 marched in a "gay pride" parade with a sign proclaiming, "I love my gay son." A minister offered her the use of his church for what was to be the first organized meeting of parents of homosexuals.

Parents FLAG has more than two hundred local chapters and information hotlines in our country in all fifty states. This organization not only offers support to parents, but also endeavors to reunite families, and is an advocate for the civil rights of lesbian and gay people and their families.

For more information about Parents FLAG, send $1 and a self-addressed envelope to: Federation of Parents FLAG, P. O. Box 20308 Denver, Colorado 80220, Attn.: Brochures. Or call (303) 321-2270.

6

Parenting*

Many things can be said about parenting: It is life, it is joy, it is pain, it is forever—whether you live with your child or not, whether you are the custodial parent, a long-distance parent, the biological parent, or the nonbiological parent. Parenting is not just a role; it is a total experience.

Gay men and lesbians who are parents have all the usual problems of heterosexual parents, and a few unique ones of their own. The same is true for their children. Counselors who work with members of these families, or their friends, must be aware of the particular stresses they encounter. There are painful emotional and social issues to be faced. Frequently, there are vexing legal concerns that these families must address. For example, lesbians and gay men are often considered to be "unfit" by the courts when it comes to raising children.

What is a family anyway? For most people it is a heterosexual couple and their children. Family Association America recognizes that "American family life reflects America's heritage of cultural and ethnic diversity. Family Service America recognizes pluralism of family form. Family Service America views the family primarily in terms of its status as a functional group rather than in terms of its form. Well-functioning families are both a building block for and a support to the larger society. Such families provide emotional, physical, and economic mutual aid to their members, assisting family members in both survival and well-being. Ideally, such families are characterized by intimacy, intensity, continuity, and commitment to their members."[2]

*Portions of this chapter originally appeared in *The Sourcebook on Lesbian & Gay Health Care.*[1]

Gay and lesbian families are good examples of significant changes in family styles that still meet the basic needs of family members as noted in the above definition. Many lesbian and gay families are made up of two adults who do not have children. A growing number of lesbians and gay men, however, are choosing to have children and are expanding the size of their family. Lesbians and gay men come to parenthood in many different ways. Some are unaware of their sexual orientation until after they marry and have children; others make a conscious choice to hide their homosexuality in favor of the more socially acceptable and respected heterosexual relationship. They frequently bear children and then are unable to continue their straight masquerade. Others, usually younger lesbian and gay men, are establishing significant relationships with their lovers, uniting to create a family and planning their family additions in a thoughtful way.

Thus there is a generation of parents who had their children before they "came out." These parents may have to deal with issues such as "coming out" to family, friends, children, and schools; privacy; possible divorce; custody and visitation rights; possible loss of a child if they choose to live with a lover; isolation and economic hardships. Some of these parents have even given up visitation and/or custody of their children out of fear and guilt.

These issues (plus many more) can precipitate intense panic involving many levels of anticipated reactions and consequences. It is important for counselors to focus on differentiating the rational fears from the irrational fears in their clients. It must also be noted, however, that it is not necessarily irrational for gay parents to fear losses.

For example:

An ex-husband may know about and be accepting of his wife's lesbianism and not be interested in having custody of his children. He may, however, change his mind and decide to pursue custody under pressure from his new wife when he remarries.

Or:

A known sperm donor who is not interested in raising his child, gets involved with a new lover who wants children. The sperm donor goes to court to obtain his legal rights to his child.

Another, newer generation of lesbian/gay parents is emerging. They are choosing to have their children after they "come out." And they do not live in the traditional heterosexual family constellation. An increasing number of lesbians are choosing to become parents. Some have a "planned pregnancy" with a sexually participating male who may or may not play a fathering role in the child's life. Others choose alternative insemination by anonymous donor or artificial insemination by a known donor who may or may not play a role in the life of the child. There are other lesbians who adopt a child. " 'It's phenomenal,' said Rhonda Rivera, a lawyer in Columbus, Ohio, who has many lesbian and gay clients. She said she knew of at least thirty lesbian mothers in and around Columbus."[3]

Gay men, until recently, generally have also had to depend on a heterosexual marriage as a way to acquire children and family. Currently, more men are mating with single women friends, who may or may not have been lesbians, to produce children.

Also, many gay men who are not HIV positive are donating their sperm to either single women or a lesbian couple who wish to have a child. In these cases, the father may have a parenting role but he generally doesn't live in the primary household. More gay men are also adopting children, especially children who are older or harder to place, as well as becoming foster parents.

Variations on all kinds of relationships are emerging. One lesbian has written a book recounting her experiences with the trio she formed while living with two gay men. This group produced a girl child who had "two daddies." The identity of the actual biological father is not known, although the mother had sexual relationships with both men.[4] Another variation can occur when a lesbian or gay man marry, have children with whom they live in a primary household together, and, in addition, have lovers outside the home whom they see on a regular basis. In some cases one may even find one lesbian couple and one gay couple living together communally and raising a child.

"A North Carolina lesbian couple, who asked not to be identified, obtained sperm from a gay man they knew. He and his lover are helping bring up the girl, now two years old. She spends one-third of her time with the men. 'For all of us, it has been a really joyful experience,' said the mother's partner."[5]

These parents also have worries. They worry about what to tell a child conceived through artificial insemination. They worry about how to deal with school and health-service personnel regarding the child's biological history and family composition. They must deal with any social stigma that may be attached to themselves and their children for being different. They have concerns about the different roles and legal rights of both biological and nonbiological parents involved with their children, whether or not they live in the primary household.

This new generation of lesbian/gay parents must also face issues related to AIDS. For example, a gay man wishing to father a child must deal with finding out if he or his lover is infected with HIV. Women who have been sexually active with or impregnated by gay men before the last several years of AIDS awareness worry if they or their children are carrying HIV. Clinicians have begun to work with fathers whose lovers or themselves have ARC or AIDS. Mothers are coming to grips with the reality of having been inseminated by gay men who are carrying the HIV. These mothers may also have been infected through their own previous sexual partners. The ultimate worry of all these parents is that their child may have AIDS or that they themselves may die from AIDS after having parented a child. Should any of these concerns prove true, huge amounts of anxiety, fear, and guilt coupled with anger and bewilderment must be dealt with.

All gay and lesbian parents must deal with their children's questions about coming from a different kind of family. For example: "Who is my father?" "Why can't I live with my father like other kids do?" "Why do I have to have two mommies?" "How do I tell my friends about your lover?" "If you haven't been divorced why are there three of you?" Counselors and friends need to be sensitive to the pressures these parents often can feel as a result of their children's questioning. Parents need to be helped to understand their children's confusion and/or conflict about coming from a nontraditional family. This is especially true in view of the lack of appropriate language to explain such situations, particularly to younger children who tend to be quite concrete and not as able to cope with abstractions as an older child might. We can see this in the following example of six-year-old Diane talking with her father:

DIANE. Are you my real daddy?
FATHER. Yes I am, but why do you ask?

DIANE. Because Sally's daddy lives with her and her mommy, but you don't live with Mommy and me.

FATHER. But Mommy and I were never married and we chose not to live together.

DIANE. Don't you like Mommy?

FATHER. Well, yes I do, but liking someone doesn't mean that you have to live with them.

DIANE. What about loving someone?

FATHER. Your mother loves Ruth and the three of you live together. I love Ted and we live together.

DIANE. Well, Timmy lives with his mother and his father lives so far away that he can only see him in the summer. That's 'cause they are divorced—are you divorced, Daddy?

FATHER. No, Diane. We are not divorced. Mommy and I choose not to live together.

DIANE. Would you have chosen to live together if you knew I was going to come along? Would you love me more if we lived together?

The children's confusions and conflicts may be different from their parents'. However, these concerns are usually related to being accepted and liked, and not wanting to be seen as gay or lesbian like their parents. Children's experiences can also trigger off their parents' homophobia, as can be seen in the following example of Amy and her son Josh:

COUNSELOR. You seem very upset.

AMY. I am. My son came home from school the other day and told me that the kids were calling him a faggot.

C. So-o-o?

AMY. That's a horrible word.

C. What does it mean to you?

AMY. Queer, gay, homosexual?

C. What did it mean to your son?

AMY. I don't know. I didn't ask him.

C. How come?

AMY. I was too upset.

C. What did you think that they were doing?

AMY. Well, I thought that maybe they were calling him that because of me.

C. I think we have two separate issues here. Kids use the word *faggot* all the time to put someone down. The first thing you need to do is separate yourself from your son and then help him figure out what was going on that would make the kids call him faggot.

AMY. That seems to make sense.

C. The second thing we need to do is to take a good look at your own homophobia and see if it is interfering with your relationship with your son.

Legal issues relate to custody questions and parental rights—not just for married couples separating, but also for lesbian and gay parents. The world of alternative insemination raises many legal and ethical questions. For instance, on the death of biological parents, grandparents have sued for custody against the nonbiological parent, who may have raised a child five, ten, or more years.

For example:

After Joanie Perlman died in 1984 her parents sued to have custody of their granddaughter Kristen, who was being raised by Janine Ratcliffe, Joanie's lover of ten years, who had been there for her prenatal development, was there for her birth, and raised her for her first five years. After two custody trials that lasted four years Judge Robert Scott (17th Circuit Court Judge in Broward County, FL) awarded final custody of Kristen to her lesbian parent Janine Ratcliffe. This decision was unusual because the judge decided that Janine was Kristen's psychological parent and that this was more important than the grandparental blood ties. This is truly extraordinary since homophobic Florida legislators passed a law in the 1960s barring gays from adopting. This legal process took a great toll on the adults involved, as the story in the *San Francisco Examiner,* June 12, 1989, attests. "'When they took Kristen I pretty much cut myself off from people,' says Janine in her St. Petersburg home, with one room for her and another, in white and blue frills, for Kristen. 'I just sort of collapsed inward and gave up.'"

After the second hearing, Rose Perlman was quoted as saying, "I can't understand how a judge could take a little girl and take her from her blood relatives." Her husband Bernard said: "We're not fit parents? And this woman is?" The words come from him a few minutes later: "She's a full-fledged dyke. But my granddaughter loves her more than anything else in the world."[6]

Mr. Perlman's statement clearly reflects and supports Judge Scott's awareness of and decision about the importance of Janine's psychological parenting role. (Initial custody had been given to the maternal grandparents, the Perlmans.)

Even further into the twilight zone of "parental rights" are the questions raised, and the problems posed, when nonbiological parents separate from their lovers with whom they have been raising children. In many cases we do not even have a linguistic frame of reference to define their roles, let alone their rights. Often, legal rights are nonexistent and the plight of these parents goes officially unrecognized. Even the lesbian community is guilty of not recognizing lesbians who are not the biological mother.

Thousands of parents have taken steps like Karen, Carol, and Bill (p. 10). In planning for their baby's conception and birth, the three consulted with a lawyer in order to spell out and protect everyone's rights as much as possible. They drew up a donor agreement for Bill, and a nomination of a guardian for minor agreement for Karen. Altogether, the three devised and signed a partnership agreement that clarified their intent to provide and nurture their child jointly, even in the event that they were no longer living together in the family home. They are using powers of attorney, wills, and contracts to achieve some of marriage's benefits and, hopefully, protections.

Unfortunately, these agreements are not always recognized legally and, since breakups do occur frequently, emotional situations are created that are not always conducive to negotiating differences. It is the counselor's or concerned friend's role in many of these breakups to be alert to and to deal with the mourning process, the sense of loss and depression that accompanies the separation for all the parties, including the child. Upon separation, visitation issues can have complicated psychological ramifications. Being a nonbiological parent often involves as much as, if not more, commitment as being a biological parent; but it does not include much social recognition, if any. It's hard to get support during a breakup if people never recognize a relationship as valid in the first place, or accept members of the relationship as parents in the second place. These breakups can deeply affect the children who may have to deal with such heartless comments as "he (or she) wasn't your father (or mother) anyway" made by an angry adult. Unfortunately many of these nonbiological parents may never be able to see their children again. This happens when the hostilities between the two lovers cannot be settled with the "best interests of the child" in the minds and hearts of both.

The children of our pioneering lesbian and gay parents are in a particularly unique spot. Like all children, the circumstances of their birth are beyond their control. While most children's sexual orientation is the same as that of their parents, that is usually not true for those of lesbians and gay men; these children tend to be heterosexual. As a result, these children can be exposed to the same societal homophobia as their parents. They often can feel homophobic about themselves as offspring of gay parents. Tragically, these predominantly heterosexual children frequently can experience homophobia toward their own parents. This situation can cause tremendous ambivalence, guilt, and anxiety for the children, as well as for their parents.

Children of gay and lesbian parents frequently fear that they may be homosexual also. It is not unusual to hear these children ask, when they feel comfortable enough to, "Am I going to be lesbian/gay like you are?" Unfortunately, not all children raise the issue. There are reasons why children may not bring up this crucial topic. They may simply feel too afraid or inhibited to voice their true feelings, having assessed that their parents are unable to tolerate any discussions of this highly charged issue.

As a direct result of their inability to talk freely about this topic and in an attempt to protect themselves, some children appear to be indifferent and quite accepting of their parents' life-style; when in fact, they may *feel* completely the opposite. Underneath, these children may consistently and vehemently protest that, I DON'T EVER WANT TO BE GAY OR LESBIAN."

Parents, in turn, out of their own anxiety, often interpret their children's lack of questions as tacit acceptance of their life-style. It is very important for parents to initiate discussion and be sensitive to the subtle openings their children may give them to talk about their feelings about having a homosexual parent or parents.

It is important that friends and clinicians help parents to

explore their feelings and anxieties about their children's possible (and/or real) negative reactions to their life-style. Parents also may need help in encouraging their children to discuss issues pertaining to the exploration of their own heterosexual orientation. If the child is heterosexual, which is usually the case, that can be as difficult on a gay or lesbian parent as it is for a heterosexual parent to learn that his or her child is gay. For some gay parents who are negatively inclined toward their heterosexual counterparts this can possibly be a more difficult period of child rearing. These parents may not be aware of the negative impact of their hostility on their heterosexual children, who may feel devastated by what they perceive as their parents lack of acceptance of them.

Alienation from peers is devastating for all of us, but particularly so for children. Information from earlier generations of children of gay and lesbian parents, now in their teens and twenties, indicates that no matter how much they loved their parent(s) as people, they still had to deal with their parents' homosexuality—sometimes with great conflict and guilt. Needless to say, it can be very upsetting to homosexual parents to feel their children's nonacceptance and anger. This is particularly so for those parents who have not realized that their heterosexual children have been placed in a coming-out situation that they understandably may resent. No adolescent wants to be different from his or her peers. This resentment rarely has anything to do with whether or not they love their parents. Rather it has to do with a circumstance (homosexuality) that is beyond their control, and that is regarded by many of their peers and society as weird, at best, or, at worst, as perverse and unacceptable.

Michael, the twelve-year-old Berkeley boy, is very clear that he thinks his mother is special, and also about why he doesn't want his friends to know she is lesbian.

"They'd probably think that 'cause my mom is gay that I was gay and that I was, like, a weakling, or whatever, you know? I'd probably get in a lot of fights," he said.

He added quickly: "'Cause I'm straight."

That nervousness is one Kevin White remembers well. White was sixteen when his father announced to the family that he was gay and moving out. There was shock. And burning stigma.

Anybody in puberty is afraid that gay parents will raise gay kids. And, yes, you worry about it, too," said White, now thirty-two, a filmmaker, and married.[7]

Another example of this situation can be seen in the following interview that involves two lesbians and their eleven-year-old son:

C. How was your vacation?

NANCY. Awful.

GINNY. It was really hard.

C. What happened?

NANCY. John wouldn't talk to us in public. He said he was embarrassed to be with the two of us together.

C. Why was that?

GINNY. John said we were the only two women there with a child. Everyone (every kid, that is) at the hotel was there with a mother and father or some other "real" relative.

C. So what did you do?

NANCY. I cried a lot. I wasn't prepared for this. My feelings were hurt.

C. How?

NANCY. He said he wished I didn't live with them.

GINNY. He was really very mad that Nancy had called him out of the pool (while he was playing with his friends) to put a T-shirt on because he was getting very burned.

NANCY. He said how dare I do that while he was playing with some new kids he had met—I wasn't his mother.

C. That must have been very hard for you, Nancy.

NANCY. It was. I don't think either one of them even realized how hard it was for me. John apologized for talking rudely, but that was not the only point. It's getting harder and harder to know what's acceptable and what isn't as he gets older, more self-conscious, and more able and ready to express his discomforts about our relationship.

GINNY. But I really felt good that he was able to speak up. I expected that something like this was going to happen.

NANCY. That's fine for you. I myself was devastated.

GINNY. I think you don't think that he loves you.

NANCY. Well, how would you feel to be told you are not his mother and have no right to tell him what to do?

GINNY. I guess I'd feel pretty terrible.
c. Well, Nancy, what about Ginny's point? Do you think that John doesn't love you?
NANCY. That's not the point. It is really hard in this kind of situation to know what to do anymore. He's very self-conscious about us.
GINNY. Nancy's right—it is getting harder but I think that the most important thing that happened was that John was more comfortable and even more affectionate after he blew up at Nancy, and we all talked about it and his feelings. I also don't think that it is an issue of love—it's an issue of appearances.
c. Sounds like it's not only a one-shot deal either. There will be plenty more to talk about as John gets older. The important thing is that you are all willing to brave the uncomfortableness and talk about it as the opportunities arise.

Many younger children of the most recently created lesbian and gay families will grow up loving their parents and accepting their nontraditional life-styles. One might anticipate some problems and pain, however, as these children begin their entry and integration into the mainstream heterosexual society where they will encounter negative attitudes toward homosexuality. In all probability, these children will grow up to be heterosexual and to live their lives in this heterosexual world or in a heterosexual manner. Balancing heterosexual values with the experiences they have in their lesbian and/or gay families may lead to conflict for them. We, as counselors and friends, must try to help lesbian and gay parents be aware of these possible conflicts and, as a result, see that their children may not like everything they do or stand for even if they love them.

Despite the bravery and dedication of the different generations of gay parents, we must remember that they are human beings who frequently have to cope with overwhelmingly painful isolation and loneliness. Being a pioneer and walking new paths, is hard work. Some of our pioneers may have difficulty recognizing, accepting, or reaching out for help. Although they may be aware of their differences from traditional parents, some gay and lesbian parents may not see how much they have in common with all parents. Frequently they are unsure from which world to seek support.

Some people who read this chapter may think that lesbians

and gay men should not have children. That is not what we are saying. All children have problems with their parents, whether gay or straight. Children have special problems with any variation from the norm on the part of their parents. Divorced parents, adoptive parents, immigrant parents, interreligious parents, etc., all create special situations that must be dealt with by the children. All we are saying is that gay or lesbian parents, like other "different" parents, have to think very carefully about the ramifications of their decisions or actions that effect the child's life in the present and the future.

Some examples of situations that must be thought about in regard to their effect on children are as follows:

(1) Instances where there are not two involved parents of the opposite sex—whether or not there are two of the same sex.

(2) Instances where the child is not involved in mainstream heterosexual activities, but limited to gay or lesbian culture, such as an all gay day care center.

(3) Situations where a child is not allowed to see the non-biological parent after the breakup of a long-term relationship.

(4) Instances where the parents do not take seriously enough or do not respect the child's right to his or her heterosexuality and his or her possible disapproval of their homosexuality. (This is not dissimilar to an interracial couple not considering deeply enough how the offspring will be accepted in our very racist society, or adoptive parents deciding not to inform the child of the adoption and thereby not respecting the child's potential need or right to know the truth about his/her unique biological heritage.)

The authors understand that making these kinds of decisions may be very difficult; the immediate results of decisions of this sort impact on the parents' issues while the long-term effects of these decisions may impact more on the children. For example, lesbian couples may choose alternative insemination because they prefer not to have a man directly involved in their lives and/or to avoid the man's later making a legal claim to the child, whereas their children may prefer to have a father in their lives to hang out with and do things with (like most of the other kids have). Further, lesbians have to consider whether to give the child information about the sperm donor in the future, and, if they do, what kind of relationships the child may have with him.[8]

For a heterosexual child (and most lesbians and gay men have heterosexual children) the lack of opportunity to form an intimate relationship with someone of the opposite sex may become problematic.

When lesbians or gay men decide not to have a member of the opposite sex involved in a parenting role, they may not consider that their child might see them as having deprived him/her of the opportunity to develop an intimate relationship with a parent of the opposite gender. In helping friends and clients plan for having their child(ren) it may be useful to help them anticipate some of the long-term effects of their decisions. It is through increased awareness on everyone's part that we are best able to attend to problems when they occur so that they will not become too overwhelming and/or destructive. It is the authors' conviction that families that thrive on communication, cooperation, and support produce moral and caring individuals who can be strengthened by change, rather than being overwhelmed by it.

7

AIDS: The Disease That Does Not Discriminate

In 1988, C. Everett Koop, M.D., surgeon general of the United States—in a nationwide mailing to American homes—declared, "AIDS is one of the most serious health problems that has ever faced the American public."[1] AIDS, which stands for Acquired Immune Deficiency Syndrome, is a disease that can affect all of us: male or female, young or old, rich or poor, heterosexual, bisexual, or homosexual. AIDS is not just an American problem; it is a world health problem. In many countries it is primarily a heterosexual disease. Seventy-five percent of the people who have AIDS in the world are heterosexual.

In the United States gay men were the first significant group of people to be diagnosed with AIDS. This unfortunately led to a misunderstanding and mislabeling of AIDS as a "gay" disease. Although gay men may have gotten the disease first in our country, they did not cause it. They "caught" it, like everyone else has, through the transmission of bodily fluids in sexual contact, the use of dirty needles, and blood transfusions.

Why gay men? Perhaps they were exposed more because many gay men have traveled to many places in the world. On October 23, 1988, the *New York Native*, a widely read gay newspaper, surveyed their readers. "One of the single most outstanding areas of discretionary spending for our reader is travel," the article said. Of their readers, 94.7 percent had taken a domestic trip in the last twelve months. In the last three years, 70.5 percent had made a trip outside the US. The average number of roundtrips was four. "43.6 percent of our readers," the story said, "are enrolled in a frequent flyer program (over 8.5 times the national average), and 67.1 percent hold a valid passport that

90

has been issued in the last five years."[2] World travel, whether associated with business or recreation, may have brought American gay men into contact with men from, or men who had visited, countries where AIDS first occurred. Since the norm had been for gay men to be sexually active and use various drugs, the stage was set for international transmission of the disease. No one knows for sure exactly how the path wound from country to country, but the disease arrived at our doorstep. The symptoms were first seen in gay men. Our first fatalities of the disease in the United States were gay men. Unfortunately, as gay men are not generally held in high regard in our country, the disease was not given, and is still not being given, the serious attention that is its due by our government, nor by the population at large.

One side effect of this discrimination was the development of a large grass-roots movement by gay men to provide care for their "brothers" who were dying at an alarmingly increasing rate. Two well-known grass-roots organizations are the Gay Men's Health Crisis in New York and the Shanti Project in California. Many broad based mainstream services have followed their lead in developing programs for HIV/AIDS patients. Chances are higher now that you may know of someone, or have a friend, or a client who has AIDS (who may or may not be gay), because the disease is spreading to the heterosexual population, and because services are more widespread.

At present AIDS is affecting not only gay men, but also women, children, blacks, Latinos, whites, Asians, American Indians, babies, adolescents, college students, etc. Much of what will be discussed in this chapter is applicable to all people with AIDS. However, in keeping with the focus of this book, we will be discussing AIDS as it affects gay men and lesbians. Our examples in this chapter are of gay men. When we wrote the book in 1989 lesbians represented a very small portion of the women with AIDS in the United States and it was generally believed that they were not at risk for HIV infection. We now know that is no longer true.

How do you get AIDS? AIDS is caused by a virus. The virus can be spread through having sexual intercourse (vaginal, anal, or oral) with an infected person. It is also spread by blood contamination from the use of dirty needles and, very rarely these days (because of improved testing), by blood transfusions.

Infected women who are pregnant can pass the AIDS virus to their babies in pregnancy or during birth. It is also suspected that mothers can pass the virus through breast milk while nursing infants.

AIDS is *not* spread by casual contact such as: using toilets in public bathrooms, touching, hugging, or shaking hands, eating in a restaurant, sitting next to someone who has AIDS, swimming in a pool, donating blood, being bitten by mosquitos—or any number of ways fearful people have imagined. You can not necessarily tell if a person has AIDS by looking at him/her. People may carry the virus and be perfectly healthy for ten years or more. Carrying the virus does not mean a person has AIDS. There is a long incubation period before any symptoms indicating immune-system problems appear. At the time of this writing, some people have tested positive for the virus and have not developed any conditions associated with the disease for ten or twelve years.

When symptoms do develop some of the more common ones include: unexplained persistent fatigue, unexplained fever, night sweats or chills that last for several weeks' duration, persistent diarrhea, dry cough, sudden and unexplained weight loss, and thrush (white spots around or in the mouth that last for weeks). In lesbians the symptoms of HIV infection can present differently since women are subject to organ specific diseases and conditions (e.g., cervical displasia, HPV, recurrent monilia, or yeast infections) unique to their reproductive organs. When any of these symptoms appear a doctor should be consulted as soon as possible.

A doctor may suggest a blood test. If the test comes back positive that means that the person has been infected with the Human Immunedeficiency Virus (HIV) and can infect others. It does not mean that the person has AIDS, or will get AIDS, although this might happen. If a lesbian suspects she has the virus it is of utmost importance to find a doctor familiar with the symptomatic pictures possible in women since so many health care providers do not consider women to be likely candidates to have the HIV infection or view, for example, their vaginal symptoms as possible indicators of HIV disease. This is largely due to the fact that the Center for Disease Control guidelines of what constitutes the diagnosis of AIDS show that AIDS is primarily understood as a white gay men's disease. Women, as usual, do not exist and the guidelines are inadequate for them and their symptoms.

Receiving a positive test result is typically a very traumatic experience for everyone, including those who do the counseling. Even seasoned veterans of this plague are torn apart by each new positive test result, as it does represent a possible potential loss of life.

In addition to encountering people who test positive for the virus, or people who have AIDS, you will also encounter another group commonly referred to as the "worried well." These are people who are medically well, yet preoccupied with the threat of AIDS and are constantly looking for, or interpreting all of their physical symptoms as signs of AIDS—e.g., persistent coughs, colds, bruises, swollen glands, etc. It is very understandable that the "worried well" exist since AIDS is so frightening, and since so many of these people have lost loved ones to the disease. It is also understandable since most, if not all, gay men are at risk for sexual behavior and/or drug usage that occurred before anyone knew AIDS existed. It is important that you are sensitive to, and respectful of, all the "worried well" you come in contact with, regardless of how irrational they may sound. If one has lost one or more friends to the disease, the fears are never completely irrational. The expression of these fears is often a beginning step toward starting to deal with the realities of the disease, both as they affect a person in terms of his own health, as well as in terms of the losses he has experienced (or is experiencing).

If taken seriously, these fears can be a vehicle to help a person start to look at the way he deals with his own health, the various ways in which he may be neglecting himself (drugs, alcohol, stress, etc.), and the ways he may take better care of himself (e.g., nutrition, exercise, rest, safer sex practices, etc.). It can also be a time when the person starts to look at the meaning of life and death and develop more of a philosophical or religious outlook on life. For example:

JIM. I've had a cold for two weeks now. I just can't seem to throw it off. I know it doesn't make any sense but I keep worrying about it.

c. You mentioned this last week too. You really are worried, aren't you?

JIM. Yeah, it is a little embarrassing because lots of people I know have colds—but I can't stop being worried.

C. What do you think is going on?

JIM. That's the problem, I don't know but I keep thinking about AIDS.

C. Do you think that's a real possibility?

JIM. I guess it always is—but no, not really. I'll just always be concerned.

C. Well, maybe it is something else.

JIM. Like what?

C. Maybe it is not as concrete as AIDS itself.

JIM. What do you mean?

C. Maybe what's happening has to do with your thinking more about how you take care of yourself and some of the risks which you take with yourself and your body.

One of the questions that is being posed for gay men, lesbians, and heterosexuals more and more is whether or not to be tested for the HIV antibody. The question of testing can come up for a variety of reasons, not just because of the presence of some of the symptoms that were mentioned earlier. Very often people think about being tested (1) because they want to know about their own health, whether they have been exposed to the virus, and whether they are possibly contagious; (2) to check the status of their blood before they donate it to a friend or loved one who might need a blood transfusion; (3) to see if they can either be impregnated or be a sperm donor; (4) to find out whether further medical treatment is needed (e.g., AZT, etc.). It is very important that the test be done as confidentially as possible, if not anonymously, because of our society's plague mentality about AIDS. Regardless of whether or not the person tests positively, this precaution is important. Frequently, just the fact that other people know of the test could cause serious problems. These problems include: social stigma, job loss, health insurance coverage problems (possibly even leading to the loss of benefits), an inability to get benefits, housing discrimination, etc.

Many people advise against testing if there are no symptoms because the process of being tested can be anxiety provoking and because there are not adequate services available to provide counseling for those who do test positive. If people test positive they can have a variety of responses. They can be totally devastated and seek out support from friends or professionals; they can be totally devastated and become socially isolated. They can be initially upset and then deny that anything is wrong with them, or they can become upset and decide that they are going to do everything they can to beat it. As a friend/counselor it is very important to remember to help your friend/client see that a positive test in an otherwise healthy person does not mean that the person has AIDS. What it does mean is that the person has been exposed to the virus and is contagious. Here you have two separate issues. The first issue is that the person is not sick. The second issue is that the person can infect others if precautions are not taken. In the discussion below Helen grapples with these issues:

HELEN. *(quietly)* I got my test results yesterday.

C. What was it?

HELEN. *(crying)* I'm positive. I have AIDS. I'm going to die. *(more crying)*

C. I'm very sorry to hear that.

HELEN. *(crying some more)* I've got it. I don't know what to do.

C. *(quietly)* I know that you are very upset. Do you remember anything from the conversation we had about the test before you took it?

HELEN. No!

C. It's understandable because you are so frightened. Maybe you can't take this in right now but I want to remind you of what you yourself told me—a positive test does not mean you have AIDS now.

HELEN. I can never make love with anyone again.

C. That is not true. You can make love but you have to use safer sex precautions.

HELEN. *(despondently)* What good will that do?

C. What do you mean?

HELEN. It means I can never have a relationship again.

C. Why not?

HELEN. Who would want to love or make love with someone with this disease?

C. Again—let me remind you—you don't have AIDS.

HELEN. *(angrily)* That's easy for you to say . . . you didn't just test positive.

C. That's true but the fact is that you don't have AIDS and that's important for you to take in.

HELEN. But I may get AIDS.

C. That's also very true. That is why it is so important for us to help you focus on the various ways in which you can start to take better care of yourself.

As you can see in the dialogue above, many feelings get evoked: anxiety, fear, panic, anger, and despair/hopelessness. These are difficult emotions not only to feel but also to work with. One example of how to handle them is as follows:

HELEN. *(after the counselor has said "this does not mean that you have AIDS" and after she has expressed a lot of hopelessness)* Who am I possibly going to turn to?

C. Right now you have just been given some news which is very frightening to you. It's unfair for either you or me to expect you to experience anything except fear, anger, or despair. What we are going to do is stick this out together.

HELEN. Really?

C. Yes. You need to know that you are not alone. While you are feeling so badly let us try to think of who you could turn to.

HELEN. Well, I do have Sue and Tina and maybe even Nancy.

C. Good! When are you going to see them next?

The counselor is joining the young woman in her anger and not trying to take away her pain. She is trying to help Helen accept the fact that she is in a difficult spot and to help her realize that she does not have to be alone. Knowing that there are people one can turn to and be with when one is feeling devastated is often the only thing a person can do to provide any kind of solace. Although it may seem like very little—feeling less alone is very healing. This is important to remember, not only when you are talking to someone who has tested positive, but also when talking to a friend or loved one of a person who has tested positive. We all have a tendency to need to do something concrete when we want to be of help. It is all too easy to forget that being able just to be there in a loving, caring way can often be the most helpful and important thing a person can do for another.

In the illustration below, a counselor is speaking to Helen's friend Nancy, who is feeling very helpless because she does not know what to do for Helen:

NANCY. I don't know what to do for Helen.

C. What do you mean?

NANCY. What do you do for someone who has tested positive?

C. What would you like to do?

NANCY. That's just it—there's nothing I can do—she's not sick. She can cook, she can clean, she can go to the grocery store.

C. What do you usually do with her?

NANCY. Go out to dinner, go to the theater, go bowling, walk around the city, rent videos, and hang out together . . . lots of stuff.

C. So-o-o?

NANCY. But is that enough?

C. Sure—if that's what Helen would like to do.

NANCY. What about talking about it? I'm afraid I'll make her feel worse if I raise the topic.

C. You could talk to her about just that and tell her how much you care and you don't want to do anything to make it harder but that you'd like to talk about it and be there for her as much as you can.

NANCY. That's OK?

C. Absolutely. As a matter of fact people often avoid talking to their friends about their illness or problems, and that can leave the friend all alone with her fears and worries.

NANCY. I get it. I could hurt us both by avoiding the topic. I guess both of us could be avoiding it by trying to protect each other. If I initiate it then at least she knows that I'm not afraid to talk about it.

C. That's right. And by doing your regular activities with each other (along with the talking) then you're treating Helen as a whole person and not as someone who has AIDS and is going to die tomorrow.

NANCY. That reminds me of what John said when he had AIDS. He used to talk about how he didn't want people to know just because it always seemed that they treated him as an invalid once they did know.

C. That's right . . . lots of times people who have tested positive and those who are sick with AIDS need to feel they are very much alive, needed and loved . . . that others enjoy their company and want to be with them. They want to focus on living.

In the example above, the counselor places an important

emphasis on being accepted and living as fully as possible. Many people get this acceptance through love, support, caring, and positive energy from their friends, family, and loved ones. People who get this acceptance seem to live longer fuller lives, despite the course of their disease. This infusion of positiveness seems to fuel a person's desire to live and fight for his/her life more persistently. This is very important to a person who tests positive, or has AIDS.

Many people respond to a positive HIV test and/or a diagnosis of AIDS with total negativity, anger, and despondency. This can happen at any time, although people typically become more accepting as time goes on. It is important for all of us to remember that the prospect of AIDS can be totally devastating. Some people can react to the news by isolating and withdrawing socially and emotionally and sometimes attempting suicide. If a person really wants to commit suicide, there is nothing we can do to stop him. If that does happen and the person is successful it can be helpful for those who are left behind to remember that a life with that disease and all of its implications was just too overwhelming and painful for their person to bear. In some cases people will attempt suicide and live and be grateful that they were unsuccessful. An example of this can be seen in the following dialogue between Mike and his friend:

FRIEND. Why did you do it?

MIKE. Because I was afraid that my having AIDS would ruin my lover's life. I thought that if I killed myself at least he would get the insurance money.

FRIEND. He wouldn't, though. No insurance company pays for suicide.

MIKE. I didn't know that. I guess I also didn't know how much people care about me.

FRIEND. It's true. We all love you and were devastated when we thought that you might have succeeded in taking your own life.

MIKE. I know that now. I won't try again. I don't want to hurt you all that way—I feel so loved.

Feeling accepted, wanted, and loved is crucial throughout the course of this disease, especially when the symptoms of opportunistic infections begin to appear—e.g., herpes, shingles, Kaposi's Sarcoma lesions, etc. The appearance of the sores and lesions associated with these conditions take away the invisibility of the disease and can cause one to become more self-conscious.

It is often not until the appearance of the external symptoms that parents learn of their children's illness (and in many cases not until a person is gravely ill in the hospital with such conditions as pneumocystic carini pneumonia (PCP), taxoplasmosis, etc.). This often happens because many men and women have not told their parents of their homosexuality before they become ill. It can also happen because many people deny the severity of their illness and because they are afraid of the stigma and possible rejection that can occur when the nature of their disease becomes known. All of these concerns do have some validity and should not be dismissed lightly when discussing them with your friend/client. Many people have been rejected when their families learned that they were gay and had AIDS. For some families it is just too much to handle at one time. They are ashamed, repulsed, and never want to have any contact with their children again.

Despite the seriousness and severity of the news that their sons and daughters have shared with them, many parents do not abandon their children. In fact, many parents come through for them in wonderful loving ways. Many travel long distances frequently to be with their sons and daughters, cook for them, nurse them, and love them. Many arrange to have their children come home to live with them until they die. Even after the deaths of their children many parents become or remain active with AIDS-related services or political organizations.

Our couple from chapter 1 is an example of how AIDS can develop and how those involved can react. That example also shows how helpful it can be to encourage those affected by AIDS, or those testing positive, to become involved with support services that are available in the community. In this case, in addition to consulting their own counselor, the couple also used the hospital social worker, as did their parents.

John and Harry (pp. 24–25) had just begun to anticipate and make plans to deal with their various needs as they were developing in the course of the disease. Further planning was facilitated and begun in the hospital. John's social worker met with him and Harry several times during John's first hospitalization. She helped them to look at their respective fears and feelings. On her recommendation, they each decided to draw up a will and execute a power of attorney so that one could act for the other if the other was incapacitated (write checks, etc.). They also decided to draw up living wills, which they had placed in their doctor's files with extra copies for themselves. They did this to avoid having extraordinary medical measures taken to keep them alive when there was no possibility of them having quality to their life—e.g., being on a respirator indefinitely, etc. In addition, John also signed the hospital's living will, which was placed in his medical chart. Beyond the hospital, they opened joint-checking accounts and signed power-of-attorney forms, which their bank required. They took these steps to protect themselves as John's disease progressed, and in case Harry should also get sick.

Very often in large communities there is a range of different services available for people with AIDS and their friends and families. This can vary from groups that provide meals for the homebound to hospices for the dying. Some groups focus on spiritual needs, some provide social activities, and some even take care of the pets of people with AIDS who cannot do it themselves, but who enjoy the company of their lifetime companions. Resources in smaller towns may be significantly more limited in scope. However, it is very important for the helping person to assist those affected by AIDS to connect with whatever resources are available. It is also important to realize that some people are going to refuse to have anything at all to do with these resources. Rather than become impatient with them, it is important to remember that maintaining one's dignity is always the key to the healing process.

Very often, denial sets in soon after a person has been diagnosed HIV positive and/or with AIDS. This is a defense that anyone directly involved with this virus will become intimately familiar with. Many of us in the helping professions have been taught that denial is one of the most primitive of human defenses. Many of us in our training have also been taught, or received the impression, that denial is something that we must cut through. In dealing with AIDS, most of us can learn to respect the defense in a way that we may never have before.

What is denial? Denial is one of the mind's ways of protecting itself from an overload of overwhelming pain, fear, or anxiety. When the mind uses denial, it enables the person to continue functioning.

Sometimes this process is not dissimilar to what happens when a circuit in the electrical system in your home becomes overloaded. At that time the overloaded circuit shuts down, while the other circuits in the system continue functioning. The significant difference here, however, is that with the circuit breaker in a home, one can just flip a switch and power is restored and the lights go back on. With a person, we cannot just flip a switch. As a matter of fact, denial is not within the person's conscious ability to control. However, denial does enable a person to continue functioning. Sometimes people may barely function and at other times they may function very happily and productively.

If the friend/counselor insists on pushing for a "serious discussion" about AIDS, he/she most likely will meet with a lot of anger and resistance. So then one might ask, "Why push it? Why not just join the person in their focus on living and enjoy the time you have with them?" For example:

JOSE. I'm feeling much better now. Going back to work next week. I've made plans to get together with friends every night this week. I've started back to the gym and I'm thinking about taking a trip to Europe in the fall with my friend Sam.

FRIEND. That's great that you feel so much better . . . but don't you think you're overdoing it a little bit? It was just last week that you could barely get out of bed. I'm concerned that you may have a relapse.

JOSE. You sound like my mother. Give me a break. Now that I finally feel good, I want to enjoy.

FRIEND. I understand. I'm just worried about you.

JOSE. That's not helpful. What's helpful is for you to encourage me and you can start by having dinner with me tonight.

FRIEND. You're right. Who's going to cook or shall we go out?

Here the friend/counselor may very well find that denial can be experienced firsthand as something positive and hopeful . . . which of course is very healing. In doing this it will be especially helpful if the friend/counselor tries to be ever aware of subtle openings that the person may give for talking about his condition. These may take place suddenly and unexpectedly. For example, you and your friend could be at the theater and during intermission while talking about the show, he might say, "I would like to see as many plays as possible before I die," or "There's one other play I would really like to see before I die," etc.

Another example could be that the two of you are having a scrumptious meal together and your friend may say, "I often wonder how much longer I'll be able to have meals like this." Surprisingly, you may find at times like these that as eager as you have thought you are to talk about the disease you respond to your friend with a statement of denial yourself, such as, "Oh, don't be silly, you're fine. We are going to have lots of meals like this," etc. Perhaps you will only be able to develop an awareness of your own tendency to denial after you have experienced making these responses several times. When you are aware of these tendencies, you can try to cure yourself of them. For example, if you hear yourself saying something like, "Don't be silly, you're going to live a long time," you can add, "Look at what I just said; it is really hard to accept the fact that you have this disease, but you do and you are right. So, let's think about and try to plan for the special kinds of needs that you have so that we can try to be sure that you can have them met."

Denial can also pose serious problems during the course of the disease. Many times you may find it necessary to take over certain areas in your friend's life, in spite of the fact that he may be very resistant and possibly furious with you for intruding into his life. Examples of this could consist of (1) taking your friend to the hospital because he is dehydrated and/or disoriented (when he just wants to stay home a little longer to rest and see if he can get better that way); (2) insisting that your friend allow others to help take care of him because of his memory loss, his tendency to fall, etc. (when your friend minimizes the importance of these symptoms); (3) emphasizing the need for safer sex practices when your friend insists that he is perfectly healthy and is of no danger to anyone sexually (see appendix I).

Most men have been brought up to believe that to be "men" they must be self-sufficient in all ways. Many gay men are very self-sufficient, successful people who are not used to being dependent on others for their care. Many of the men who are testing positive are in the prime of their life and have never experienced any serious illness. They are proud of their bodies and the good shape they have kept them in. Physical appearance is very important to them.

The emphasis on the physical may create unique kinds of body-image problems for gay men with AIDS. Any marring or altering of their body through loss of weight, loss of hair, lesions, etc., is an extreme blow to their ego—which often causes them great difficulty in going out in public.

EMORY. How do I look?

HATTIE. You look good.

EMORY. No, no. How do I really look?

HATTIE. Well, you're thinner, but otherwise you look OK. Your clothes are too big on you, though. Why don't we get you some outfits that are your size.

EMORY. No, no. I'll gain weight soon.

HATTIE. I'm sure that's true, but in the meantime let's have you look as good as you can so you'll feel comfortable going anywhere you want. It's enough already that you have this disease. Why make it harder for yourself?

EMORY. OK. Will you help me?

We all have to be sensitive to the possible loss of personal autonomy involved when we think of care giving. Although we may be well intentioned, it is important not to reassure people automatically about their appearance. It is essential to be aware of how self-conscious people can become and how painful it is to go through the changes associated with the course of the disease. These changes can cause a complete readjustment to one's self-image, both in terms of physical appearance and physical abilities. Also, each new manifestation of the disease that takes place in a person with AIDS can force him/her to acknowledge in an increasingly more profound way that there really is something wrong. This will happen for you too.

ALBERT. I don't want to use a cane. Everybody will know that I have AIDS.

ALICE. They will know that something is wrong and they will be right—there is something wrong. But they won't know you have AIDS.

ALBERT. But I'll look like an old man. I'll feel foolish. I'd rather stay inside.

ALICE. OK. I know it's hard. Why don't we do this? You haven't been able to walk in three months. Let's just practice walking indoors and see how it feels. Maybe you'll get more comfortable with it.

Maintaining a sense of personal dignity for your friend/client is an important goal to remember throughout the course of the illness. This is something the friend/counselor can "do" in a philosophical sense as opposed to a physical action. For example, acknowledging that staying in and resting has an important value in itself, even though you might be inclined to think that it is more important for your friend/client to go for a walk outside. The value of the maintenance of this respect is especially true as the disease progresses and your friend/client becomes more dependent on others for care.

One of the more frustrating and confusing aspects of AIDS is the wide variation of mood swings and sense of physical well-being that people experience. For example, one day your friend/client may seem quite chipper and the next day extraordinarily flat, depressed, and fatigued. Pain may be excruciating for several days, causing you to think your client is soon to die. Then suddenly, for what may seem like no reason at all, he will seem just fine. Especially during the initial phases of the illness he may be nasty, impressively unappreciative, rejecting, and totally obnoxious. This can be absolutely devastating for those with whom he comes in contact.

Friends may encounter different situations from counselors. Friends may be asked or expected to do more favors of a "personal" and possibly more time-consuming nature.

For example, you may find that your friend sends you out to do some shopping for him every time you visit. You are eager to do this for him because you are very concerned about his not eating. Anything that you can get him makes you feel better. You are as preoccupied with food for him as he is, and yet you are finding that the time you set aside to be with him is being taken up with food shopping. So, rather than just be an errand person, you tell him that this is getting frustrating for you because you do not get to be with him. You can tell him that you are more than happy to shop for him but that from now on you will only get him things if he asks you ahead of time when you call to arrange to come over. He may not like this and you may have to repeat it a few times and follow through. There may be some scenes if he does not get what he wants when he wants it—at these times you may find it necessary to tell him that you may find it necessary to leave if he continues to be abusive and you may have to leave to illustrate your point—always telling him when he will hear from you next so that he does not get the impression that you are deserting him forever.

You may have to keep repeating your messages to your friend as some people with AIDS develop memory loss that may affect their understanding on either a short-term or permanent basis. Because memory loss is often a factor, you cannot always rely on your friend to initiate a discussion of what he would like you to get him at the store. A good rule of thumb is to ask when you call and possibly suggest that you pick up some things that you know he likes. But even with preparation on your part, your friend or client may just be obnoxious.

At these times you may feel angry and furious and want nothing to do with him. However, in your love, committedness and compassion and with your deep sense of helplessness, you may feel compelled to be as accepting, cheerful, and positive as possible, and quietly take the abuse. Meanwhile, the person who is ill—out of his own sense of resentment and anger and also entitlement (since he believes he is dying and may—as so often is the case—resent you for being healthy and having a full life ahead of you)—may continue to make demands on you. He may possibly berate you for not meeting those demands. This tends to happen especially in the area of food. At other times, your friend/client may be responding in a negative or apathetic way. This may simply be a result of physical pain or other effects of his illness and he may not be aware of the way in which he is treating you. As these things take place, you will learn to appreciate what the Step Programs (AA, Al Anon, DA, etc.) mean when they refer to "taking it one day at a time." Here you will, in all likelihood, find that you are taking one moment at a time— changes can take place that quickly!

In your compassion and your efforts at being helpful, you may not realize that your friend or client who is ill probably has no idea at all of the impact his behavior is having on you; he will not have any understanding of that unless you let him know. This may be very hard for you, because you don't want to cause him to have any more pain than he is already experiencing. However, if you just let time go by in the hopes that he will once again become considerate, you may find that your resentment has become so great that you really cannot be there for him. Therefore, it is very important for you to try to speak up when you find that you are getting fed up, hurt, and/or abused.

AIDS has been and continues to be a very confusing disease. Although we have no cure for it, increasingly we have been able to find more ways of prolonging people's lives through the use of a wide variety of medical treatments. Because of the appearance of more medications to treat opportunistic infections, people with AIDS are living longer and having longer illnesses than they did before. This can and often does lead to more complicated medical care situations, multiple and continuous hospital stays, long term home health care experiences and hospice complications. You may have difficulty dealing with the unpredictable ups and downs of your friend's illness. Throughout the course of your friend/client's illness you may find that you feel very awkward about talking directly about the fact that he/she does have AIDS. There is no easy answer for this. Many people believe that it is important to have deep emotional conversations with their friends who have AIDS before he/she dies. In reality this is more of an ideal than the norm. In our society death continues to be a topic that is difficult to acknowledge and discuss openly. Painful feelings are evoked by the subjects of death and dying. It takes a special kind of strength, acceptance, and inner peace for dying persons to talk about their impending death with others. This is also true for the people they are talking with. The vulnerability and intimacy involved can be very scary for everyone. It is the authors' belief that no one has the right to decide how another person should deal with dying. After all, whose life is it, anyway? This is a very individual matter. No one is the same. Each of us has to find his/her own path. Some people will always be in denial—right up to the moment of their death. That is all right. It is their life—it just makes it harder for us. Conversations that we consider to be so important, while they can help both people feel closer, are not always possible.

Helping a person to die can be a very emotionally painful experience, as well as a very beautiful and fulfilling one. Frequently the relationship two people have with each other deepens and grows as their time shortens. Moments become precious, as do a gesture, a word, or a touch. Times can be quiet and they can be active.

We have not talked about the various medicines, the hospital procedures, the decision-making process about where to die (hospital, home, or hospice), or funeral arrangements. These are universal constants connected to illness and death. They are topics that one can raise at all points during anyone's illness. Although they may seem morbid, they can provide a means for getting closer and talking about the meaning of life.

You may have many specific questions that we have not answered. We have tried to share some of what we have learned in our own personal experience with AIDS. This experience is an intensely emotional one. The varied, multiple, and often-painful diseases associated with AIDS seem to bring human suffering to a new height, both for the person with AIDS, and those who love and care for him/her. But we are also aware that people need specific information about medical, legal, religious, financial, and other resources. In anticipation of this we have included an extensive reference list at the back of the book.

We will, however, mention one unique way to memorialize those people who have suffered and died from AIDS. The AIDS Memorial Quilt is a symbol of love and remembrance that has been made by thousands of friends, loved ones, volunteers and supporters of the NAMES Project, a grass-roots organization that documents the lives lost in the AIDS epidemic. Inspired by the American folk art tradition of quilting and sewing bees, the Quilt not only includes names and dates, but also personal memorabilia of each of the persons remembered on every three-feet-by-six-feet fabric panel.

When the Quilt was first displayed in October 1987 on the Capital Mall in Washington, DC 1,920 names were read and the 1,920 panels that made up the Quilt were unfurled. In 1988 the Quilt returned to Washington, only this time it was composed of more than 8,000 panels and it had been seen by over one million people. On October 6, 1989, the Quilt again returned to Washington and this internationally known memorial to the tens of thousands who have died of AIDS was unfurled again so that people could understand the value of those lost lives of men, women, and children. By the time the Quilt reappeared in Washington during October of 1992 over 20,000 panels commemorated the ever-growing number of fatalities from this hideous disease.[3] For further information, contact the NAMES Project, P.O. Box 14573, San Francisco, California 94114.

8

Older Lesbians and Gay Men

Aging in our society is most typically anticipated and experienced as something to be feared, dreaded, mourned, and generally avoided as much as possible. With our orientation toward youth and youthfulness, we have creams to take out wrinkles, dyes to "ungray" our hair, operations to remove or tighten sagging skin, makeup to hide old-age spots, etc. Very little emphasis is placed on the positives that come along with advancing age such as the development of wisdom, the recognition of our limitations, and the development of more realistic expectations of ourselves that can help us lead fuller and significantly less frustrating lives. In addition, there can be a deeper appreciation of life that focuses more on the moment and the joys of being alive than on the future, the need for acquisitions, and the assumption that our bodies will never wear out and that our health will always be good, no matter how we abuse ourselves.

As one grows older, one has the opportunity to appreciate and value the miracle of good health and the miracle of life in such a way that our lives can be full and complete, even if our hearing is going, our eyesight may be lessening, and our bodies need the aid of such helpers as insulin, pacemakers, new heart valves, hip and knee replacements, etc. The loss of many loved ones can often help us learn that life cannot be taken for granted. It can also help us look at and seriously ponder the meaning of life and death in a way that we have never done before. The experience of various successes and failures that we encounter and that those we love encounter can help us to develop or gain a sense of patience, an appreciation of change and of process that we never experienced when we were young.

108

As this maturing takes place, we have the opportunity to focus on living our lives in as meaningful a manner as possible. In experiencing a fuller life, we also can begin to comprehend the place of death in our lives—recognizing that death is an inevitable part of life that can come at any time . . . sometimes with forewarning and sometimes not. We learn that death is not a punishment, but rather a conclusion.

Older lesbians and gay men exist in all walks of life. Some are, or have been, married. Many are not only parents but also grandparents. Some live in urban areas. Others live in rural areas. Some are rich and some are poor. Some have planned for the future and some have not. Some are angry and bitter while others are at peace with themselves and the world. Some are in long-lasting relationships, while others have been single most of their lives. But, whether or not they have been in intimate partnerships, older lesbians and gay men tend to have developed and belong to support groups that consist of friends, neighbors, business associates, and relatives. Some of the people in the support groups are straight and some are gay. Some have shared their life-style with many people and others have shared it with a select few. This human resource network is a valuable asset for older homosexuals because it frequently helps to prevent many of those "horrors of aging" that so many people fear out of their belief that older gay men and lesbians are not in relationships, do not have friends, and descend—as they grow older—into a life of despair, aloneness, bitterness, depression, and isolation.

Actually, the reality is very different from what many people imagine for older lesbians and gay men. Although some do fit the "depressed and isolated" stereotype, there are more who do not. Lesbians and gay men have a unique situation in that the very stigma they have experienced for their life-styles has also prepared them to deal with the stigma associated with aging. To begin with, this has forced them to look to their own resources as an individual; this is not as true for older heterosexuals who have most likely been able to look to their families of origin and their families of procreation for the support they need. When that support is lost to them, heterosexuals often do not have a supportive friendship network to fall back on, as lesbians and gay men do. Lesbians and gay men, who have not tended to form traditional family groups, have most often had to learn how to depend on themselves. This is an important attribute that is not always developed in our society, even though it may be given lip service.

We can see this most clearly in the case of older heterosexual women who were often raised to look to their spouses to provide for them financially and to make the major decisions for the family. These women focused their life energy on taking care of others while minimizing the importance of taking care of themselves and, in general, did not tend to see themselves as capable, self-sufficient people. They frequently became lost or displaced when their children left home, when they divorced, or when their spouse died. This is not as true for older lesbians who have had to take care of themselves (and often their children) ever since they "came out." They have learned to support themselves financially (whether they are in a couple or not), to become self-reliant, to arrange for their taxes to be done, to plan for their future, and to anticipate for their financial needs when they are older.

Older gay males have an advantage over older heterosexual men in that they have not been taken care of by a woman most of their lives. They have had to learn how to cook, clean, iron, shop, do their own laundry, make their own social arrangements, etc. Many heterosexual men have depended on their wives for these services. They often become overwhelmed and feel helpless at the loss of their wives through divorce and death. Their need to develop basic independent living skills can create serious adaptation problems for them at an advanced age. It can also make the mourning process that much more difficult and possibly prolonged.

Another aspect of life where older lesbians and gay men may fare easier than heterosexuals is in the area of physical appearance. Many female heterosexuals grow up with a strong emphasis on physical beauty and youthful attractiveness as a prerequisite for getting, having, and holding a partner. This may not be as true for lesbians, who tend to place more emphasis on personality, intellect, and the commitment to a lesbian identity. Since lesbians place more of an emphasis on the person as a whole and on the quality of relationships in general, loss of physical attractiveness through aging tends not to be as significant and traumatic as it might be for the heterosexual woman.

This also applies to the ability to find a new lover later in life. Since women live longer than men, it may be much easier for a lesbian to find another woman than for a heterosexual woman to find a new man.

Gay men seem to stress the importance of physical attractiveness almost as much as heterosexual women do. They are concerned about their appearance and work hard to maintain a strong body through working out in gymnasiums, lifting weights, etc. Many participate in individual sports such as tennis, running, scuba diving, swimming, etc. The anticipated loss of physical attractiveness may cause some to be fearful of the aging process, although studies have shown that this is not necessarily so. The studies of Kelly, Sagir, and Robbins, and Jay and Young found that "only a minority of the gay men expressed an apprehensive attitude toward aging. For that minority, the apprehension was usually based on fears related to an inability to attract a sexual partner (physical appearance), loneliness and being alone."[1] The authors' experience in their practices and friendships is somewhat different. They have observed significant "middle-age crisis" in many of their gay male friends and clients.

There are some special and unique issues for lesbians and gay men, however. One has to do with whether they identify themselves as homosexual or not. Many older lesbians and gay men were fearful of "coming out" when they were younger and have remained so throughout their lives. This lack of being able to talk openly about their lives is very oppressive. It is also socially and emotionally isolating. Closeted older lesbians and gay men do not talk about the important life incidents with others while older heterosexual men and women are free to share these events fully. This can be seen most poignantly when the loss of a loved one occurs for a homosexual person and the mourning process remains a secret because of the nature of the couple's relationship and the fact that it was never publicly acknowledged. For closeted homosexuals, this lack of sharing could cause a deep depression and a prolonged mourning experience that might not be recognized by others for what it really is.

Older heterosexuals can and do talk freely about the loss of their loved ones. These relationships are considered valid and important in our society. Homosexuals who are "out" have a better chance of adapting to their losses because of the existence of their friendship network in the gay community (and, often times, in the heterosexual community as well). Homosexuals who are "out" to a select few also fare better than the closeted homosexuals. An example of the importance of being able to share with others appears in May Sarton's book *Recovering*.

Ms. Sarton writes very poignantly about her companion, who is on a visit from her nursing home:

> I need to commemorate with something better than tears my long companionship with Judy that began thirty-five years ago in Santa Fe and ended on Christmas Day. Now I am more alone than ever before, for as long as Judy was here at least for the holidays and even though only partially here, as long as I could re-create for a few days or hours a little of the old magic Christmas at 139 Oxford Street and then at 14 Wright Street in Cambridge, I still had a family.[2]

In working with older people it is often difficult to know whether that older person is lesbian or gay. There is not a particular look or outward means of identification. As a matter of fact, many times older people are not even seen as sexual, much less lesbian or gay. Who even thinks of sexual-orientation issues or questions when taking a family history of an older person? Who thinks of sexual orientation when planning for day-care treatment or nursing-home care for an elderly person? To help us listen more clearly, it is important that we each be as aware as possible of our biases both around aging and around human sexuality.

Many older lesbians and gay men have developed a way of interacting that is unique to their generation and invisible to most other people. They often have long-term relationships where they never openly refer to one another as loved ones. They often have a strong social network with others who are similar to themselves.

In connection with this we would like to share a small vignette. A friend of ours had to go to a funeral on the West Coast. When he came back he was very excited. He told us that the funeral brought together many of the older people in his family and he found out some interesting information. "I found out that there are at least six of us in the system." Our friend proceeded to tell us about the man who came from Washington and the woman who came from Iowa. And then there was Joan from Texas and Bob from New Mexico and he was living with, you know, that roommate schoolteacher for the past fifty years, or something like that. What was so fascinating was the absolute lack of any identifiable words about sexual orientation in their conversations about themselves and their loved ones.

Yet the knowledge was there that these were probably lesbians and gay men if you listened to their language carefully. Language is important because older people use words such as *friend, dear friend,* or *roommates* to refer to lovers, because they really do not identify themselves as homosexual. They may love someone of the same sex but would never talk in terms of sexuality or sexual orientation. They would be very offended if others referred to them as lesbian or gay.

In the following conversation one can see several nontraditional clues that the friend/counselor may or may not respond to.

C. Do you have any children?

MARY. No.

C. Have you ever been married?

MARY. No.

C. Have you always lived alone?

MARY. No. I had a roommate for twenty years. She just died last year.

C. Were you close?

MARY. Yes. We went on all our vacations together and shared many interests.

C. Have you tried to get another roommate?

MARY. I have thought about it. It would help out financially, but it just would not be the same.

C. Why?

MARY. Because my roommate was very special to me. No one could replace her.

C. It must have been a terrible loss for you.

MARY. Yes, it was. I feel very alone these days. Not many people knew how important Emily was to me.

In this example the counselor, in learning that Mary had no children and had never been married, could have become concerned with Mary's lack of involvement with a man, thinking that she was a "pathetic old maid." Instead, the counselor listened and followed Mary's lead and focused on the relationship that she, herself, described as primary.

However, there may come a time in Mary's life when the counselor will need to communicate with her in a more direct way. Suppose Mary does get another roommate and this person becomes ill in a hospital or is dying in a nursing home. How will Mary visit her friend if the institution insists on a family member's only policy, as so many do? The friend/counselor will have to be able to discuss the issues involved in as nonhomophobic a way as possible, as well as act as an advocate for Mary, so that she can be with her "friend."

The friend/counselor will also have to be aware of the particular importance that a will, a living will, and a power of attorney have for the aging lesbian or gay man. These are very difficult topics to raise with anyone; for some reason most of us in our society have learned that it is offensive and possibly even hurtful to raise any issues that have to do with anticipated illness, death, or dying. Yet it is especially important for lesbians and gay men to do so as their relationships are not recognized as legal. It is not unusual for family-of-origin members, e.g., brothers, sisters, children, or even grandchildren, to ignore the significance or even the presence of a lover in their relative's life.

Many horror stories exist about the losses that a lover of many years can experience when relatives ignore and devalue the existence of his or her relationship. Surviving lovers have lost homes they shared for many years with their deceased lover when relatives contested wills. They have even lost the funds the couple shared in their joint bank account when their lover's relatives have seized possession of their deceased lover's assets.

These stories highlight the importance for lesbians and gay men to establish their relationship as solidly as possible—both through legal documents and through word of mouth by talking to their doctors and lawyers about their concern that their significant other or lover be allowed to make important decisions about their lives at any time that they might become physically or mentally incapacitated. Legally, this can be done through documents such as a power of attorney and a will. When talking about a power of attorney it is very important for the friend/counselor to know that a document drawn up by an attorney and the persons involved will not necessarily be universally recognized. For example, hospitals and banks may have their own forms that they require their patients or clients to fill out. Such organizations as credit bureaus and insurance companies will in all probability recognize and accept the power of attorney drawn up by a lawyer and his/her clients, but it is always safer to verify this with your own company. (Of course this information applies not only to the older generations, but to people of all ages.)

We know a man we shall call Harry, who, upon realizing that his lover was becoming senile, went to the bank and talked to the officer with whom they had dealt for many years. In his conversation, Harry learned, much to his distress, that the power of attorney that he and Sam had drawn up many years before was not considered valid by the bank, which required that their own forms be used. Fortunately, Harry was able to have Sam sign one of these legal documents during a moment of lucidity. The bank officer knew about the importance of the relationship that existed between Harry and Sam and was more than willing to accept the newly signed paper.

Harry and Sam were very fortunate. In many areas of our country the prejudice against homosexuals is so strong that even the most obvious evidence of a long-term relationship between same-sex people will never be recognized as valid. This can be a most painful and costly denial of the "reality" of the nature of a relationship. It clearly exemplifies the need for the friend, or person in the helping profession, to be able to advise his or her clients accordingly.

Although we have talked about some of the differences between the older lesbian and gay male and the heterosexual, the reality is that these two groups have a lot in common. Both are concerned about their health, the quality of health care that is available to them, and financial security. It is very important for each group to have a sense of independence and the opportunity to live life as each chooses as long as each is able. A sense of dignity is of utmost importance, as is self-respect. Family and friends are looked to for reassurance and support. For many, contact with those who can provide spiritual guidance is helpful.

As life draws to its conclusion it would seem that the differences between homosexuals and heterosexual people diminish somewhat. Not that they disappear. The differences begin to blend together as all older people deal with the process of bringing their lives to an end as fully as they can.

9

Alcohol and Substance Abuse in the Lesbian and Gay Communities

Many people in the gay and lesbian communities consider alcohol abuse and other drug usage to be one of their most serious problems. According to statistics that were quoted in *Our Voice,* a publication of the Pride Institute of Minneapolis, Minnesota—the first drug-treatment center in the United States to serve lesbian and gay men exclusively—33 percent of the gay and lesbian population is chemically dependent, compared with the 10 to 12 percent of the general population having drug or alcohol problems.[1] One might deduce from these statistics that there is a causal relationship between homosexuality and alcoholism or drug abuse. This is not true. What is true is that there are pressures in society as a whole and within the lesbian and gay communities that can increase lesbian and gay men's susceptibility to alcohol and drug use or abuse.

We live in a society where substance use is seen as acceptable by a large percentage of the population. Whether you pop pills for pain, drink alcoholic beverages to "feel good," or spray away your nasal discomfort, the message is clear: there is no reason to be uncomfortable or experience pain. In our society everyone is expected to be happy and feel good. This is a message that we are given whenever we read a newspaper or magazine, listen to the radio, or watch television. We are a nation of self-medicators and if we are unable to find a substance to make us comfortable, our friends and neighbors are all willing to suggest their favorite remedies. We will even use our friends' prescriptions when they are offered to us.

Children start drinking at a very early age, younger than most of us know or want to believe. It is not unusual for sixteen- and seventeen-year-old people to join Alcoholics Anonymous. This includes lesbian and gay youth as well. Clearly the message reaches us at a very early age that drinking provides an acceptable way to relax, be freer, and be more social. This is often supported in our own homes where we watch our parents take a drink before, during, and after dinner, serve alcohol to their friends and have a drink when they are upset to help them calm down. Some of us may also have witnessed our parents taking various sorts of pills, smoking marijuana, snorting cocaine, etc.

Lesbians and gay men come from these families just like everyone else. As they have grown older they, too, may have engaged in this behavior. In addition, lesbians and gay men experience stresses that are unique to their life-style that they often try to minimize by the use of alcohol and/or drugs. It is these very stresses that lesbians and gay men use as rationalizations when their substance use begins to become substance abuse.

These stresses can begin to take place when one first becomes aware that their sexual preference is for someone of the same sex. During this time, alcohol may be used in many different ways. One of these ways is trying to ease stress as one tries to deny same-sex feelings while attempting to continue in intimate relationships with members of the opposite sex. Another is to help deal with the anxieties and excitement incurred in the process of "coming out" to one's self and to others. A third might have to do with helping one deal with the pressure of "being in the closet," which typically causes tension and anxiety. And, finally, a fourth reason for drinking or other substance abuse has to do with the various forms of discrimination, rejection, oppression, and fears of emotional and physical attacks that all lesbians and gay men experience at some time in their lives.

When the use of alcohol and other substances is rationalized away by emphasizing the terrible, painful stresses in their lives, lesbians and gay men do themselves a great disservice. They may say, "Who wouldn't want to medicate away these pains?" That is just part of the denial,which is very harmful to people with addictive behavior. It is clear that working through the acquisition of a lesbian or gay identity requires a clear head. This means a head free of alcohol or drugs.

Lesbians and gay men do not have access to the variety of opportunities for socializing that many heterosexual people have. The lesbian or gay bar has traditionally been the "safe" place where people could meet and socialize, even if they do not drink. Bars also serve as information centers for what is taking place in the lesbian and gay communities. They provide a place for people to network. They are a setting where people can neck, hold hands, dance, and have physical contact. They are also a setting where lesbians and gay men do not have to be afraid of discrimination, which could be the case if they were in a straight bar.

Urban areas have more bars specifically for lesbians and gay men than rural areas (which may not have any). Typically, there are many more bars for gay men than for lesbians. In more rural areas there are fewer people to support gay or lesbian bars. Because of this, one often finds that the rural bars that do exist are mixed, serving both lesbians and gay men. In some rural areas one may find that there are no bars that exist for lesbians and gay men. However, among those that do exist there may be those bars that serve both nongays and gays together. Gay men and lesbians are less anonymous in these settings and many feel more threatened. If this is the case, they may find that it is wiser to attend a bar out of town in a more distant metropolitan area.

In dealing with friends or clients who are lesbian or gay, people have tended to suggest bars as a primary place to meet others. This is especially so in the case of gay men; lesbians do not use the bars as frequently as gay men do. Unfortunately, this perpetuates the exposure to the use of alcohol and the dependence on the "bar scene" as the primary way for people to meet others and socialize. It is important for us to become more familiar with the variety of resources that exist in our immediate and surrounding areas as alternatives to the bars. We may accomplish this by asking the lesbians and gay men we know, calling lesbian and gay hot lines, reading gay and lesbian newspapers and periodicals, and calling the local Alcoholics Anonymous. As a result, we may find resources such as restaurants, gay professional groups, gay religious groups, as well as sports groups (bowling, running, volleyball, softball, hiking, etc.). We may also find lesbian and gay AA (Alcoholics Anonymous), ACOA (Adult Children of Alcoholics), and Al Anon meetings.

A friend/counselor may have the following type of exchange with a person with whom he or she is dealing:

WALTER. I don't know what to do. I'm so lonely. The only place I know to go to where there are other guys like me is the bar on Sycamore Street. But that's no good 'cause I always drink too much.

C. Have you asked any of the people you have met at the bar about other places to go?

WALTER. Yeah! But they are too far away.

C. What about places other than bars?

WALTER. What do you mean?

C. Aren't there any places other than bars that you could go to?

WALTER. I never thought of that. Like what?

C. Well, you are a Catholic, aren't you? What about Dignity?

WALTER. I've heard about that. Actually, last night one of the men at the bar was talking about a picnic that Dignity was having. I did not know what it was. It just sounded like some oddball thing to do to me.

C. Is this somebody you know?

WALTER. No, but he always seems to be at the bar. Maybe I'll go again tonight and ask him about Dignity.

Another example is Gail from our first chapter. As you may remember, Gail had a serious drinking problem that her friends were very concerned about. She had been blacking out and getting abusive towards others when she drank. Gail was complaining to her counselor about not knowing of places to go to socialize other than the bars. Here her counselor was faced with a dilemma. Which was more important: to focus on the fact that Gail had a drinking problem or to focus on her need to find some other place to socialize? It would be very easy for the counselor to feel sorry for Gail if she (the counselor) viewed Gail's alcoholism to be a direct result of being oppressed by a homophobic society that pressured lesbians and gay men to meet only in the bars. Clearly, this is a view that Gail would be encouraging out of her own sense of being a victim, her need to deny, and her ability to manipulate others into viewing her situation in the same way as she sees it. For example, something like the following conversation may occur:

GAIL. You just do not know what it is like.

C. But I would like to know. Tell me.

GAIL. It's awful. There just isn't any other place to relax, to be yourself, than at a bar. Everyone in my town hates gays. They are so conservative. You should hear the shit I take on the job because I am the only woman who works there. I know that they all think that I am a dyke. They do not say it, but I know that it is true. I can't talk to any of them. The pressure is just too much. I work hard and I do my job. What keeps me going all day is the knowledge that I will have a drink with my friends after work.

Here the counselor can really sympathize with "poor, pathetic Gail" or decide to help her deal with her alcoholism, even though she realizes that Gail may be resistant and possibly may become very angry. It is imperative that the friend/counselor help Gail deal with her alcoholism. Until Gail is able to do that she will not be able to make any changes in her life, because her alcoholism will just be too powerful. The counselor might proceed as follows:

C. Gail, I hear how difficult your life is, but from everything that you have told me, it is your drinking that is really causing you problems.

GAIL. What do you mean?

C. You look forward to socializing with your friends at the bar every night but your drinking is out of control.

GAIL. What do you mean? I can control it. I can stop whenever I want.

C. Have you ever tried?

GAIL. No, it is not that much of a problem.

C. What about your blackouts and the fights that you have been having with your friends?

GAIL. But that's just been happening recently.

C. When it started is not the issue. The fact that it happens at all is the problem. Are you concerned about the blackouts and the fights?

GAIL. Well, yeah. But I just have not known what to do about it.

C. How about no more drinking?

Very often people in the helping fields tend to overlook the importance of alcoholism. It is difficult to understand why this is so. Perhaps one reason is that drinking is such an accepted fact of life in our society. Another could have to do with the counselor's desire not to "insult" his/her client by suggesting that a drinking problem may exist. Finally, a third reason could have to do with the fact that alcohol and drugs have been such a significant part of the lesbian and gay social scene that the use of these various substances is taken for granted and not necessarily considered as anything unusual. Therefore, one can anticipate that the lesbian and gay client will not even think to raise alcohol and/ or drug use as a subject for concern. It is very important that the friend/counselor be aware of the need for a discussion about alcohol or drug use/abuse and be ready to enter into a dialogue when the opportunity arises.

Some people believe that alcoholism and drug use are symptoms of underlying psychological problems. Their method of helping a person would be that of focusing on the psychological problems as opposed to focusing on the drinking or drug use or abuse. They would not get frustrated or upset with their friend/ client's alcohol/drug use because that would not be their focus. It is their belief that once the underlying psychological problems are resolved, the drinking/drug use/abuse will also become resolved. An example of this approach with Gail might be the following:

GAIL. I have such a headache today. I can hardly think.

COUNSELOR. What do you think could be causing your headache?

GAIL. I don't know. I did close the bar last night with my friends. We had a great time. But I guess I drank too much.

C. Why do you think you drank so much?

GAIL. I always do. I need to drink to be able to be social and relax.

C. Let's try to understand what it is that makes you so uncomfortable when you are in a social situation.

Another approach to alcohol/drug use/abuse is that in which the friend/counselor is of the conviction that no help can take place unless and until the person has stopped indulging in or using a particular form of substance, alcohol, drugs, or pills. This is the belief held by Alcoholics Anonymous and many people in the mental health field. Many who hold this belief will not work with a substance abuser unless they are also in a program such as AA, Alateen, NA, etc. An example of how a person of this conviction might interact with Gail can be seen in the following:

GAIL. I always do. I need to drink to be able to be social and relax.
COUNSELOR. What do you mean—you need to drink?
GAIL. Just that!
C. That makes no sense. You have a serious problem. You are addicted to alcohol.

Sometimes, after you work with a person for a while, you begin to see openings in their resistance where you can explore options with them. For example, when the counselor makes a recommendation to stop drinking (for what seems to be the hundredth time) Gail replies:

GAIL. Why do I have to stop drinking? I'll just cut down.

As you can see, Gail is very resistant. This is not unusual. Few alcoholics or drug abusers are eager to give up their alcohol or drugs. In order to do this, they first have to become uncomfortable, concerned about, or frightened of the effect that the use of their substance is having on them and others. It is very easy for the friend/counselor to be available with concern, good advice, and suggestions about what to do. It is much harder to bear with the resistance, denial, and rationalizations—all impressively strong defenses.

Substance abuse in the lesbian and gay communities is three times greater than what exists in the heterosexual world. That is alarming. Lesbians and gay men must begin to look at this abuse, even if it makes them or their friends and counselors uncomfortable. Sometimes we as helpers do not realize that we may hinder exploration of these sensitive issues, but we can.

In her article entitled "Substance Abuse and the Lesbian and Gay Community: Assessment and Intervention," Barbara G. Faltz, RN, MS, points out how people who help others can inadvertently become enablers. An enabler is generally a person who condones continued substance abuse. Faltz lists twelve behaviors as examples of professional enabling. They represent a means by which to increase your sensitivity to some of the ways we can collude with our friends/clients:

1. Minimizing or not talking about the abuse or the results of it.
2. Avoiding confrontation.
3. Making excuses for continuing drug or alcohol use such as, "If you had this lover, job, parents, etc., you'd drink, too."
4. Saving the client from feeling the results of his/her addiction.
5. Trying to "protect" the client from alcohol or drugs.
6. Viewing alcoholism or addiction as a weakness or moral issue.
7. Viewing alcoholism or addiction as a symptom of an underlying emotional problem, acting out neurotic behavior, or a method of coping with life's stress.
8. Viewing alcoholism or addiction as the result of an oppressed, homophobic society that forces gay men and lesbians to meet each other only in bars.
9. Trying to find the cause and hoping that the disease will go away when insight emerges.
10. Encouraging the use of "will power" and cutting down of use for those who no longer have the option of controlled use, or seeking other oversimplified "cures."
11. Expressing anger, frustration, blame, or disappointment toward the client who continues to use drugs or alcohol despite your best advice.
12. Gossiping about the client to others, or feeling victimized by him or her."[2]

Understanding the process of enabling can make it easier for us not to do it.

Many people who help others are unfamiliar with the range of drugs available in our society for recreational use by both the general and lesbian and gay male populations. That does not mean that we cannot listen for indications of drug or alcohol use and/or abuse and, when appropriate, ask questions of people to find out if or how much they use drugs or alcohol, as demonstrated in the example below:

COUNSELOR. Karla, you talk about how lonely and isolated you
have become. How shy you are. How hard is it for you meet
new people?

KARLA. Very hard.

C. At one time you were more social, weren't you?

KARLA. Yes.

C. What I don't understand is what happened to change that.

KARLA. What do you mean?

C. Something must have happened to cause you to be less social—something other than breaking up with a lover.

KARLA. Yeah! I got scared about my use of drugs and booze, so I
decided to stay by myself—that way I wouldn't be tempted.

C. You know, you never mentioned this before. Tell me more
about it, will you?

KARLA. What do you want to know?

C. Well, how much did you drink? What did you drink? What
kind of drugs did you use?

It is not only helpful to know what drugs people use, but also
what they are used for. Luis Palacios, a psychotherapist and
drug-treatment specialist in New York City, stresses that "many
people use different drugs simultaneously, or at different times
in their lives to address different feelings."[3] According to Palacios it has been discovered that the use of particular drugs
corresponds to certain emotional states:

Narcotics (heroin and other opiates) and hypnotics (Valium and
Quaaludes) are often deployed against feelings of shame, rage,
jealousy, overwhelming anxiety. Stimulants—cocaine,
amphetamines—are used to mitigate depression, helplessness, and
a sense of inner emptiness. Psychedelics—LSD, mescaline, disco
drugs such as MDA and Ecstasy—address boredom, apathy, de-
tachment, isolation. Alcohol is often used to medicate intense guilt,
self-punishment, loneliness, longing.[4]

Many gay men have begun to examine their use of drugs and
alcohol in their efforts to take better care of themselves and in
the hopes that this will help protect them from getting AIDS.
This newfound concern over the use of alcohol and drugs is
related to the connections that have been made between drugs

and AIDS. It is not just that shooting drugs is one form of transmission of HIV. It is widely believed that there is a connection between the use of poppers (amyl and butyl nitrites) and Kaposi's Sarcoma. In their efforts to protect their patients, many physicians are advising against the use of such drugs as marijuana, cocaine, alcohol, and amphetamines.

Gay men are increasingly more concerned about safer sex. They realize that drugs and alcohol help to lower their inhibitions; that is why they have been using them. However, they also realize that if their inhibitions are lowered they will be more tempted to participate in unprotected and unsafe sex. Many gay men have decided to avoid going to bars completely because of this concern. Many will avoid any form of intimacy with those who do drugs or a combination of drugs and alcohol because of their feelings that they cannot trust them. Many are trying to lessen or curtail their own use of drugs and alcohol because they do not trust themselves with others when they are under the influence. In exploring the issue of alcohol and drug use, it is very important that the friend/counselor listen not only to the concern that the person has about other people, but also concerns he may have about himself.

In working with gay men, the friend/counselor needs to listen with a "third ear" for those topics that do not come up. Every helping person needs to listen for unspoken subjects and take responsibility for raising these issues to a conscious level for discussion. In advising gay men, drug use and its relationship to AIDS may be one of those unspoken areas of concern.

We have presented some information about alcohol and drug use and abuse. We have not given any examples of how one might introduce this topic when it has not been raised by the person with whom you are working. The following segments of interviews might be of help:

c. Alan, you've talked a lot about your friends' use of drugs, but it occurs to me that you have never said anything about your own use.

ALAN. I just use them recreationally.

c. What does that mean?

ALAN. Just socially.

c. What is just socially?

ALAN. You know, when you are entertaining, when you're making love, when you go to concerts or movies, when you go dancing.

C. It sounds to me like you must do a lot of drugs since I know from our conversations that you participate in those activities frequently. You are very social.

ALAN. That's true. I like having a good time.

C. Do you always use drugs when you have a good time or in order to have a good time?

ALAN. Usually—That's what we all do.

C. When else do you use drugs?

ALAN. Before I go to bed, when I'm home alone listening to music.

C. When don't you use drugs?

ALAN. When I go to work.

C. Do you think that your use of drugs ever interferes?

ALAN. No!

C. What drugs do you use?

ALAN. Different ones.

C. Like what?

ALAN. I smoke pot. I do a little coke.

C. What's a little?

ALAN. Maybe a line a day.

C. What else?

ALAN. Sometimes I do poppers. Sometimes "ludes." Depends on my mood and what's available. Mostly I just drink.

C. What do you drink?

ALAN. Mostly scotch and wine.

C. How much?

ALAN. Two or three drinks a night.

Another example concerns Jane:

C. Jane, I have noticed the last few times we have talked that you have had difficulty keeping your train of thought.

JANE. I know. I guess I am just tired. I have been working twelve hours a day.

C. That must be very hard for you. But I wonder if something else might be involved.

JANE. Like what?

C. Well, oftentimes people use things like pills to help them stay

awake. They they take something to help them relax, to go to
sleep . . .

JANE. Well, I have started to take pills to help me stay awake.

C. What kind of pills?

As you can see from the above examples, some people can be
engaged directly and oftentimes without too much resistance. At
other times you may encounter a great deal of resistance as seen
in the example of Gail.

Up until now, we have talked about alcohol and drug use and
abuse. We have not talked about the recreational use of these
substances. The reality is that there are people who can and do
use them with moderation and control. These people are not to
be confused with those for whom these substances present a
problem. As with everything else, it is important for the friend/
counselor to be aware of his/her feelings about the use of alcohol
and drugs so that they will not interfere with the counseling and
the relationship. It is always important to ask enough questions
so that you can make a distinction between recreational use and
abuse. When the use of substances starts to take over and interfere with one's life and functioning—when it begins to be in
control of the person rather than the person in control of it—
that is when recreational use has changed and ceases to be "fun."
That is when it has become a problem.

10

Special Need Groups within the Lesbian and Gay Communities

Lesbians and Rural Gay Men

Because many large American cities have significant lesbian and gay male populations that are not necessarily hidden (like San Francisco, Seattle, Minneapolis, St. Paul, Boston, and New York) people may tend to assume that most homosexuals live in urban and suburban areas. This is not necessarily so. Much of the United States is still rural and many of our urban and suburban lesbians and gay men have come from these areas. It is hard to ascertain really how many live outside the major metropolitan centers. However, if we were to assume that for every homosexual who comes to the city another stays home, we might find that at least half of the lesbian and gay male population still lives in rural areas. This can be problematic for many reasons.

Small-town living can cause many difficulties for lesbians and gay men because of the social, political, financial, and religious constraints within these communities. Rural living tends to be conservative and places a strong emphasis on "traditional" morals, values, and behavior. Not only is it "right" to get married, but everyone is expected to do so. Once one has married, it is expected that one will raise a family and participate in extended family activities. Clearly, lesbians or gay men who do not get married will stand out and draw attention to themselves by being different. If a person's difference was thought to be connected with homosexuality, which is considered sinful and totally unacceptable to many rural fundamentalists, he or she would not be made to feel welcome in the church.

Keeping a secret takes a lot of energy and can put significant strain on one's coping mechanisms and sense of well-being. Anonymity is hard to preserve in a small town. Anxiety can go up for many who are keeping their homosexuality a secret and levels of paranoia can be very high. People can feel very badly about themselves when they have internalized their community's negative and often-misinformed attitudes about homosexuality. This could often lead to self-hate or depression. It can also lead to isolation.

Rural areas have tended to receive fewer health and social services than urban areas and there is even more of a dearth of appropriate social, educational, and health services for lesbians and gay men. Few, if any, services are to be found specifically for lesbians or gay men. Part of this may be caused by intolerance of differences and lack of appropriate resources. Even if there were some resources that a gay person might utilize, she/he may not do so out of fear of self-disclosure and possible retribution. These fears have a realistic base as privacy and confidentiality are hard to maintain in rural America. It really can be like living in a goldfish bowl when you consider that most people in a small town usually know all or a good part of your comings and goings, who your friends are, when you have company, who they are, when your company leaves, etc. The same is true for when you go to a doctor, a dentist, or a counselor—be they through public auspices or in private organizations. Even in these settings, lesbians and gay men can have reason to question their anonymity because many staff members (both professional and nonprofessional) tend to gossip about anyone or anything that is different or controversial. This situation is compounded by the fact that many gay male or lesbian professionals who may work in the system are also affected by the fear of loss of job security and may be afraid to "come out" on the job or advocate for services for gay men and lesbians.

We have tried to describe some of the problems encountered by rural gays. The existence of these problems does not preclude some rural homosexuals making a healthy adjustment to being lesbian or gay. Some do and some do not adjust. Some migrate to other geographic areas where being different creates less pressure for them. For those who do choose to remain in rural America and wish to seek our help, it is again important that we not only be aware of our own biases and prejudices, but also have realistic expectations about what may or may not be possible for any given lesbian or gay man to achieve in her/his community.

Particularly for those of us who are most familiar with life and resources in urban areas, this has to be a priority. We may find that it is necessary to do more outreach than we are used to doing, to do more basic education on what it means to be lesbian or gay and keep abreast of current resources that people can utilize in their self-exploration. One may have to do more telephone interviewing and/or home visits because distances can be so far and time and transportation less available. We cannot stress enough focusing on realistic expectations. One may be able to walk into a lesbian and gay bookstore in a big city without fear of reprisals. Just buying or owning a book on homosexuality for a rural homosexual could be a major step for them. It could also be very threatening since someone might see them make the purchase or notice the book in their home.

The following newspaper article, reprinted in its entirety with permission from the *San Francisco Examiner,* illustrates some of the problems annunciated earlier:

Up Close in Iowa
A Rural State Confronts Reality

By Elizabeth Fernandez
of the Examiner Staff

"Everyone forms their own opinion; you have to fit in their
little cubicles"

Volga, Iowa—Here, in this century-old town where house locks rarely see the turn of a key, where durable fields of corn and oats stretch boundlessly on the flat horizon, the world outside with its unbecoming concerns and pesky problems seems very distant.

Volgans—all 310 of them—like it that way.

Then one gay man, the only gay man hereabouts, forced this town to confront reality. And Volga rebelled.

Sean Lamphier, born here twenty-eight years ago, wanted to create a hospice for people with AIDS on his 360-acre farm handed down from his grandparents.

The plan set off an explosion of fear last summer. Lamphier received death threats. Shots were fired at his car—once when he was behind the wheel. And there were threats to torch his farmhouse.

"We'd just as soon keep it away from us and our children," says Bless Coonfare, one of the local dwellers.

Lamphier, now the town outcast, was forced to give up on the hospice. But Volga, like countless other small towns across America, can never force Lamphier back into the closet. Nor can it lock out the prodigious change all around it.

In larger cities throughout Iowa, gay men and lesbians are winning acceptance and civil rights, even the near-passage of a gay rights bill this year by the state legislature.

Gay men and lesbians, who long shared Lamphier's closet, are becoming more visible, gaining a sense of community and of self, building support services and educational seminars.

"Iowa is rural by nature. We've always been a state that likes to say those people don't exist here," says Claire Hueholt of the three-year-old Gay and Lesbian Resource Center in Des Moines. "We like to be the perfect example of a nice, innocent state. But we're starting to see changes."

Those changes are turning towns like Volga into virtual anachronisms.

Tucked into Iowa's northeast, this village is home to a Bible-proud people with four mainline churches and one mobile troupe of Jehovah's Witnesses.

"To be gay and to live here is absolute isolationism," says Lamphier. "I kept it a secret for many years. I was afraid of retaliation. And I proved myself right, that I have good reason to be afraid.

"Living around here, you walk a tightrope. Everyone forms their own opinion and you have to fit in their little cubicles: white, religious, definitely heterosexual, married, two kids."

His idea for the AIDS hospice, to be called Nova House, didn't fit into one of those cubicles. According to Lamphier's plan, those infected with the fatal HIV virus would spend a week or a month soaking in the tranquility of the farm he shares with thirty-five beef cattle, sixty chickens, and a horse named Heidre.

Volga rebelled. Betty Puffett of Puffett's Hardware says the outsiders would tax the local waste-treatment plant. She also says medical care is available "not that far away." The nearest hospital is seventy-five miles from Volga.

"We're educated enough to realize that we don't need that problem here," Puffett says.

Only a few residents publicly supported the hospice.

"This is hillbilly country," says one supporter, Chuck Smith, a Lutheran minister who moved here four years ago from Minnesota. "It is homophobic. They think that basically only gay people get AIDS. Their attitude is as long as they can keep gay people out they can keep out AIDS."

Like many others here, Jane Donlon, forty, was brought up in the German-Lutheran tradition and taught that homosexuality was sinful. Today, she neither condones gay life nor condemns it, but thought the hospice was a good idea.

"It is a typical small, rural Bible town," says Donlon, a registered nurse and mother of three. "The people around here are very conservative. There is only one life-style that is acceptable, which is heterosexuality."

That was the norm for other cities in Iowa, too. Then, two years ago, Dubuque held its first gay pride parade. It drew thirty marchers, who were pelted with rocks and eggs by onlookers.

The next year, five hundred gays and lesbians marched in Dubuque's parade. And one bystander was arrested for "possession of eggs."

Dubuque and three other Iowa cities are now considering an ordinance prohibiting housing and job discrimination against gays.

In Des Moines, the state legislature this year considered a gay rights bill that, if passed, would make Iowa only the second state, after Wisconsin, to outlaw discrimination against gays. To the astonishment of gays, the bill was championed by several mainline church leaders. To their greater astonishment, the Iowa House in March approved the bill, 57–41.

While the measure died in a Senate committe in April, the House victory persuaded the gays to fight for Senate approval next year.

More than anything, the bill made gays more willing to come out.

"It is a difficult place to be gay, they have a legitimate fear of losing their jobs," Hueholt says. "Until this year we have not had many people coming out, but both the Senate and the House were bombarded with letters from people who for the first time were saying they were gay."

The transformation has turned the decade-old Gay Coalition of

Des Moines from a primarily social organization into a largely political one, though it lost several dozen members in the process.

"There are a lot of people out there in the boonies who are satisfied with the situation and don't want us to rock the boat," says Rich Joens, thirty-seven, president of the 130-member organization. "But more and more people are now willing to be public. . . . We had been talking with the straight world about our issues and hoping for a change, but it didn't happen. So we realized we have to take it into our own hands."

Still, change comes slow for many gays.

One businessman in Cedar Rapids says disclosing his sexuality would drive away all his customers. The man, who asked to be identified only as Edward, wants to sell his business and move West, away from what he calls the Midwest's pervasive homophobia. Iowa has become all the more intolerable for him since he lived in San Francisco for a time.

"The thing I loved most was the freedom," he says. "I was totally shocked the first time I saw two guys walking down the street holding hands. I didn't think there was any place on Earth that you could do that. It was like walking into paradise."

In the Midwest, he says, people "are now just reaching the stage where they will accept a boy and a girl living together without being married."

With 120,000 residents, Cedar Rapids has only one gay bar, The Warehouse. It has no signs outside, only a small neon cocktail glass.

A few years ago, Roy Porterfield was beaten unconscious with a pipe as he was walking into the bar. Despite the beating, despite being fired from two jobs for being gay, the thirty-eight-year-old car stereo installer is optimistic about life in Iowa.

"I'm out of the closet and I've never had a hate phone call or a piece of hate mail for being gay," he says. "Iowa is pretty mellow. There is a prevailing attitude to get to know people. And when you know people, it is hard to have a mindless prejudice against them."

* * *

"I kept it a secret for many years. I was afraid of retaliation. And I proved myself right, that I have good reason to be afraid. Living around here, you walk a tightrope."

—Sean Lamphier[1]

Married Lesbians and Gay Men

The idea that an individual may be married and have feelings for persons of their same sex does not often occur to many people. Marriage and heterosexuality are seen as synonymous, just as homosexuality is associated with being unmarried. Very little thought is ever given to the idea of bisexuality, even though many single and married lesbians and gay men consider themselves bisexual and not gay.

Lesbians and gay men have married for a variety of reasons. Many were not aware of their homosexuality at the time of their marriages. Many were aware of their same-sex attractions, but were too fearful of societal pressures and social ostracism to act on them. Some married because of their need for acceptance and possibly their hope that the same-sex feelings would disappear after their marriage. Others married because of a desire for a traditional family with children. They married their husbands and wives because they loved them. Another factor that has influenced lesbians and gay men to marry has had to do with numerous negative stereotypes of gay life-styles that often did not portray homosexual relationships as loving or intimate.

In a recent study by Norman L. Wyers that involved sixty-six homosexuals (thirty-four men and thirty-two women) who were either married, separated or divorced, lesbians gave the following reasons for marrying: "the expectations that they would marry, 38.2%; love of spouse, 23.5%; pregnancy, 17.6%. In contrast, gay men cited love of spouse as the most important reason, 34.4%; expectation of marriage, 28.1%; and pregnancy, 18.8%."[2] Wyers's study also says, "Male homosexuals reported greater marital satisfaction (56.3%) than did their female counterparts (29.4%). The most serious problem cited by lesbians (47.1%) was basic incompatability. A majority of the men (65.6%) cited their homosexuality as the most serious marital problem."[3]

Leading a double life can and often does cause great stress for the homosexual spouse. "I thought that I was probably the only married gay in the whole world and that all I would accomplish by being gay was that I would alienate myself from both the straight and gay societies; and I was amazed as I uncovered more and more married gays. So that made me feel more comfortable. I thought I would really be unique: be looked upon as a freak, you know.[4] Same-sex feelings may be a source of guilt, shame, and self-hate. Secret feelings such as these may lead to emotional and/or sexual dysfunction in the marriage. Another source of guilt, shame, and possible anxiety comes from clandestine same-sex interactions outside the marriage that may or may not be compulsive—that is, the person may or may not be able to stop them.

There are many examples of people who have same sex feelings and who are married. The dialogue below with Fred illustrates one. Fred is a thirty-four-year-old man who has been married for ten years and who has two children, ages five and seven. He was aware of his homosexual feelings when he married, but hoped that marriage would help them go away. He loved his wife when he married her and never told her about his homosexual feelings. He secretly sought out sexual contacts with strangers in parks, bathrooms, and movie houses, never telling his wife. Two years ago he met a man in a bar who has been actively pursuing him. He still has not told his wife because of his hope that his love for her and the children will help him overcome his temptations. Fred sought out counseling to help him deal with his guilt and in the hope that it would help him give up his homosexual feelings.

FRED. I want you to help me stop being attracted to men.

C. Tell me what you are talking about.

FRED. I can't stop thinking about men but I want to be able to think about my wife.

C. What are your feelings about men?

FRED. They always turn me on sexually. I can't stop fantasizing about them.

C. What about your wife?

FRED. That is my problem. I love her dearly. She is very attractive. She is a wonderful woman. She is a great wife, you could not ask for a better mother. Sex with us is OK, but I really prefer a man. I am much more comfortable in the company of men. I feel freer and safer, but I cannot leave or hurt my wife. I do not know what to do about her or my children. I do not want to hurt them but I really think that I would be happier if I could be with a man.

How do you think you would feel listening to this person? What would your thoughts be? Do you know? Maybe you would find yourself becoming angry at Fred for being so confused and at the way he was deceiving his wife. Maybe you would want to change him. Maybe you would have a need to make things more comfortable and think, "If I could just help him stop having these feelings about men everything would be OK." Or you might find yourself thinking, "Oh my God, what do I do now?" You don't have to do anything. All you have to do is listen compassionately and help your friend/client learn how to listen to himself. You cannot be expected to know what the outcome will be. If you think you should know, then you may try to influence your friend/client's progress according to your own agenda. The most important thing is to be in touch with your own feelings and needs so that you realize what they are. If you are able to do this you will be much better able to listen to your friend/client and help him/her define their own feelings and needs.

Another example of a married spouse is Jeanne, who did not know that she had same-sex feelings until her three children had grown into adolescence. She had not been happy in her marriage for many years. Three years ago she met Beth while doing business at her local bank. Jeanne discovered as her relationship with Beth developed that she had strong emotional and physical attachments towards women. As her relationship with Beth deepened, Jeanne remembered crushes she had had on her classmates and teachers while she was growing up—realizing that they had more significance than she had thought at the time. Jeanne eventually divorced her husband without telling him of her relationship with Beth.

Many married lesbians and gay men have children. Frequently this is the reason they do not tell their spouses about their same-sex feelings. Women tend to be afraid that they will lose their children. Men tend to be afraid that if the information were known it would have a negative influence on their children. In Wyers's study, "Gay fathers tend to be more reticent about telling their children about their sexual orientation. More than 94% of the children of lesbian mothers knew about their sexual orientation, as compared to only 46.9% of the children of gay fathers."[5] Wyers's study also indicates that most of the children of lesbian mothers lived with them on a full time basis (53 percent). That pattern was true for only approximately 10 percent of the homosexual fathers. Those statistics are linked with dissatisfaction about custody arrangements: "35.5% of the gay fathers expressed such dissatisfaction as contrasted with only 3% of the lesbian mothers."[6]

Because of the invisibility of gay and lesbian spouses, most of us know little about these people and their families. The *San Francisco Examiner* noted on Sunday, June 25, 1989, that "On November 1, 1972, ABC aired 'That Certain Summer' a sensitively acted, lovingly directed (by Lamont Johnson), often frustratingly cautious made-for-TV movie about a divorced man groping for a way to explain his gayness to his fourteen-year-old son. 'That Certain Summer' was TV's first serious non-stereotypical portrayal of homosexuality and the film's strengths and shortcomings form boundaries that, with few changes, still exist today."

It has taken seventeen years for another positive media presentation to come along in the form of the *Tracey Ullman Show* where a precocious teenage girl named Francesca is being raised by her divorced dad and his lover. This is the first TV series presentation of a gay couple as nurturing successful parents.

In addition to invisibility there is a serious lack of any kind of information about married lesbians and gay men. Married homosexuals may receive less attention from either the straight or gay world because they do not have full membership in either group. Many specialized service centers for lesbians and gay men do not usually address the special problems of married or divorced homosexuals. Since many of these people remain invisible when they seek help from many traditional agencies their plight continues to remain a secret.

In his article entitled "Bisexual and Gay Men in Heterosexual Marriage: Conflicts and Resolutions in Therapy," Eli Coleman explains that with present-day knowledge, there is no clear model for the married man with same-sex feelings who wishes to maintain his marriage. Based on his clinical experience, he suggested that some facts that seem to be important ingredients of successful adjustment might include:

1. Both people love one another.
2. Both people want to make the relationship work.
3. There is a high degree of communication in the relationship.
4. Both people have resolved feelings of guilt, blame, and resentment.
5. Physical contact is necessary.
6. The wife has a sense of worth outside the marriage.
7. If there is outside sexual contact, the wife does not know about

it, or the husband and wife have worked out an open-marriage contract.

8. The wife is willing to work on understanding and accepting her husband's same-sex feelings.
9. The husband continues to work on his own acceptance of his same-sex feelings.[7]

The most important fact to remember is the need for understanding. We all should remember that people have the right to determine the course of their lives, and it is not our responsibility to change the course or the direction they travel in. Our role as caring friends or supporters is to help them understand their choices and to assist them to enhance the journey in as many ways as possible while always remembering that they will also have to deal with the stigmatizing effects of homosexual activity.

Third World and Minority Lesbians and Gay Men

The authors have approached this section with some concern because even though we have minority memberships (women and lesbian), we are still members of the dominant white middle-class majority of our society. We have tried to be aware of our racism, sexism, and classism. We realized when we set out to write this section, that although we may know what it is like to be female and members of a sexual minority, we do not know what it feels like to be a member of a cultural or racial minority. We do not know what it may feel like to be rejected both by one's culture of origin and by the dominant culture one lives in when one "comes out." What we do know is that working with and understanding third world/minority lesbians and gay men involves the acquisition of many levels of specific cultural knowledge: the culture's gender role expectations for men and women, the attitude of that culture towards homosexuality, the importance of family (nuclear and extended) to that culture, the role of socioeconomic and educational factors and the primary identification of your friend/client—whether to his/her ethnic group or sexual orientation.

There is a limited amount of research and documentation of information that exists specifically for third world/minority lesbians and gay men. How many of you know of or have read articles about lesbian or gay American Indians? (We are using the term American Indian rather than Native American because "American Indian is the preferred term of Indian communities and organizations."[8]) What about Latinas and Latinos? How about Asian lesbians and gay men? What about black lesbians and gay men? It is important for each of us to be acquainted with specific information about many cultures since each group has its own unique ethnic, cultural, and gender differences. The life experience of a Latina is different from that of a black lesbian or gay man. These experiences differ from those of Asian or American Indian gay men and lesbians. It is essential not to generalize from one group to another.

Unfortunately, in our society the uniqueness of each group is not appreciated. Third world minority groups are seen and treated subordinately. This subordination exists on many levels: racially, economically, politically, and culturally. Perhaps an example will illustrate what we are trying to convey. In our country, the American Indians were here before we were and even taught us how to survive when we did get here. We took their land and we often depicted them in our textbooks as savages, without acknowledging the contributions they had made to our culture and that they fought to protect their people and their homelands from us. We have devalued their culture and imposed ours on them. In her article entitled, "Beloved Women: The Lesbian in American Literature: An Overview," Paula Gunn Allen (herself an American Indian) wrote the following:

> Much of modern society and culture among American Indians results from acculturation. Christianity has imposed certain imperatives on the tribes, as has the growing tendency to "mainstream" Indians through schooling, economic requirements, and local, state, and federal regulation of their life-styles. The Iroquois, for example, changed the basic structure of their households after the American Revolution. The Americans determined that they had defeated the Iroquois Nation—though they had not even fought.[9]

For the most part we, the intruders to this country, made and have continued to make, little effort, if any, to understand the values and culture of the American Indian. This is typical of our society. Despite the fact that we have a constitution that states otherwise, white Americans are very intolerant of differences. We seem to believe that we are superior. This is most clearly evidenced in the history of black people in our society who were seen, and still are seen by many, as being inferior. We fought a bitter war in this country in the last century over the enslavement of black people. Abraham Lincoln may have freed the slaves in the Emancipation Proclamation, but that did not eradicate human prejudice and, bias. Martin Luther King, although he accomplished a great deal for the Civil Rights Movement and raised our consciousnesses, was killed for his efforts to bring about social change. Despite his efforts and those of many others (including white people), prejudice toward black people is still very strong.

In working with black lesbians and gay men it is important to realize that they are members of several minorities. For example, a black male has to contend with all of the ramifications of being black, and a member of a low socioeconomic group before even beginning to deal with the implications of his homosexuality. A black lesbian has the additional burden of being female.

Since membership in the black community is so important, many black lesbians and gay men often do not "come out" to many people because of the fear of being rejected by their own community. This fact, coupled with the knowledge that they do not fit into mainstream society, can further cause them to stay "in the closet." Being rejected by both their culture of origin and the mainstream culture may be too difficult to tolerate. As we discussed in chapter 1, this was a primary concern for Isaiah, not only in terms of his social and familial needs, but also in connection with his professional ties to the black community.

Mays and Cochran, in their survey of black lesbians, noted the following:

Black lesbians, in contrast to white lesbians, may be more likely to remain a part of the heterosexual community, maintaining relationships outside of the lesbian population. This may happen for several reasons. First, black community values emphasize ethnic commitment and participation by all members of the community. Second, the relatively smaller population of black lesbians (a minority within a minority) puts more pressure on these women to maintain their contacts with a black heterosexual community in order to satisfy some of their ethnically-related social support needs. Third, black lesbians may contribute much needed financial and informational resources to their families of origin. This assistance may be critical for the maintenance of a reasonable standard of living. In contrast, for white lesbians, there may be a sufficiently large lesbian population (a similar minority, but drawn from a larger population) from which to derive most ethnic/cultural, social and emotional needs. Also, distance from family of origin may be more achievable for a greater percentage of white lesbians due to greater financial resources within the family system. Thus, black lesbians may find that the need to juggle family of origin demands and their lives as lesbians is somewhat more complicated.[10]

Friends and counselors, when dealing with black lesbians and gay male friends and clients, need to be very much aware of their lack of information, their use of stereotypes, their prejudices, as well as their attitudes toward homosexuality. Counselors of all colors need to be more aware of, and sensitive to the issue of white superiority as it exists in our society for everyone. Acosta has indicated that third world people, including counselors, may also possess these characteristics.[11]

Many of us call people who come from the third world Spanish-speaking countries Hispanic, although the people from such places as Cuba, Mexico, Puerto Rico, and the South American countries prefer to call themselves Latina (female) and Latino (male). New York and San Francisco have large populations of Puerto Ricans. Many Cubans have settled in Florida and along the East Coast. Mexican Americans are primarily found in the Southwest. Many refugees from Latin America are heavily concentrated in the South and the Southwest. Latinos live in many parts of our country.

Puerto Rican culture rejects lesbianism and homosexuality, as do many other of the Spanish-speaking areas mentioned. Puerto Ricans also struggle with racism, sexism, classism, and colonialism (despite the fact that they are United States citizens). For all of the Spanish-speaking minorities, the emphasis in the United States has always been on Anglicizing them through language and education, and on devaluing their culture of origin. If you are helping a Latino, it is important to remember that he will be looking for signs in you not only of homophobia, but also of racism, classism, and other prejudices. He may want to know how much you know about his culture, whether you are interested in learning about it, and how much you are able to appreciate the differences that exist between the two of you, as opposed to what you have in common. He may also be suspicious and, possibly initially, hostile because of previous experiences that he may have had with others where the emphasis has been on conformity and a desire for him to change, as opposed to an acceptance of him for who he is.

Another factor that you will encounter in working with Latinos has to do with the male and female sex roles that are emphasized in their cultures. For example, Luis, our Latino adolescent from chapter 1, received a suggestion from his mother to see the youth worker at the community center because she was concerned about his being so isolated. Luis did not follow through on the suggestion because it contained a contradiction to his socialization as a Latino male. Luis could not depend on a counselor and still feel that he was a strong male. In order to be a strong male, he felt that he was supposed to be able to solve his own problems and take care of himself at all costs.

So far in this section, we have talked about various types of information that it would be important to be aware of in order to help in our work with third world friends/clients. Our intent is to alert you to possible areas or indications of prejudice that might come up that have nothing to do with homophobia. For example, if you are white and your friend/client is black, you might want to say something like the following:

"You have never mentioned anything about the differences that exist between us. I wonder what it is like for you, a black man, to be working with me, a white Anglo-Saxon woman?"

or

"I have been thinking about you a lot. In reviewing the experiences you had growing up in your family, I find that I may not have an adequate appreciation of your experience because I do not know enough about your culture. Could you tell me more about what it was like?"

As we have pointed out throughout the whole book, one of the most important aspects of helping others is being aware of our own strengths and weaknesses, our biases and prejudices and how they might affect our efforts. In our interactions with third world and other minority people, it is especially important to be aware of, and open to, what we do not know. It is also important to be able to appreciate, to be curious about, and to accept differences in others. We all need to recognize the special impact that each culture, with its specific norms and values, has on us as we grow up and continues to have on us, as we go about living our lives in this ever-changing world..

Differently Abled* Lesbians and Gay Men

Perhaps the lowest position on the ladder of special groups within the lesbian and gay communities belongs to those who are differently abled. This is also true of their position in society as a whole. Ours is a society that emphasizes and places a high value on mobility and physical activity: walking, jogging, running, tennis, biking, swimming, etc.

While those who choose not to be physically active may be criticized and questioned by others, those who cannot participate are often scorned and discarded as useless. Those with disabilities are also feared both because their presence causes those of us who are able-bodied to realize that "this too could happen to us" and that we cannot take our able-bodiedness for granted. To avoid these feelings of discomfort and/or guilt, we tend to avoid contact with those who trigger these feelings off in us. We avoid people with disabilities.

One may define a disability as an impairment in one's functioning. Disabilities may be physical or mental. Some are visible, such as a spinal-cord injury or an amputation. Some are not, such as deafness or schizophrenia. The degree of disability depends on the degree of impairment in functioning.

Within our society there is a belief that differently abled people have no sexual feelings or desires and/or are incapable of

*Many of those with disabilities prefer to be referred to as "differently abled" rather than disabled. In recognition of this fact, the authors will use the term *differently abled* in this section of the book. *Differently abled* is a more positive term that emphasizes ability, whereas disabled is a more negative term that emphasizes lack of ability.

being sexual. This belief applies to all differently abled people whether they are heterosexual or homosexual. This can be particularly devastating since often there are no connections between a disability and a person's sexuality and sexual feelings. They do, however, affect one's ability to communicate with others both in general and more specifically about sexual feelings. When a disability does affect one's sexual feelings (as in neurological impairment) that does not necessarily mean that a person cannot be sexual. What it does mean is that a person with these limitations has to be creative and find other ways to achieve the desired results. For example, men can use penile inserts to achieve an erection and women can use manufactured jellies to replace natural lubricants in the vagina if they have spinal-cord injuries. Unfortunately, many of the people with disabilities have internalized the myths that exist about changes to themselves and believe that they cannot be sexual regardless of whether they have had their disability from childhood or acquired it later in life. Many people with disabilities need to be educated not only to the fact that they can be sexual, but also to the techniques that will help them achieve sexual satisfaction.

Being lesbian or gay and differently abled creates a multitude of problems for the people involved. Not only do they have to cope with society's depreciation of them as humans because they are not "whole," but they also have to cope with society's devaluation of them because they are homosexual. Their status as lesbians or gay males in the homosexual community does not make them any better off since gay people are subject to the same prejudices towards physical disabilities as straight people are. As a result, differently abled lesbians and gay men are (or can be) isolated and truly "men and women without a country or a place to belong." They are isolated not only from other lesbians and gay men, but also isolated from other differently abled lesbians and gay men. The isolation is not only a result of attitudes, but also the widespread problem of a lack of physical accessibility. For example, many buildings, to say nothing of sidewalk curbs, have no accessibility for people in wheelchairs. The financial limitations that typically exist for minority groups can and most typically also affect lesbian and gay organizations. Poorly funded groups rarely can afford "accessible" office or meeting spaces.

Those who are working with the differently abled lesbians and gay men need to look at their own feelings and attitudes about physical disabilities. It is important that the physically abled friend/counselor not assume that he/she knows what the problems of the differently abled people are. Each person with his/her disability has his/her own unique set of problems and needs. It is also important for the friend/counselor to realize that it might be hard for a differently abled person to talk freely and express feelings of anger, hurt, etc., because he/she is most often used to having been treated as inferior by the able-bodied.

When possible, it is most helpful to work with differently abled lesbians and gay men in groups. The use of the group modality allows for more exposure to others who share similar life experiences. It can also provide for the opportunity to have one's thoughts, feelings, and responses validated by others. Having differently abled counselors can be additionally valuable. Not only can they provide a positive role model but they also might be able to empathize more readily with the position of being an outsider in a physically abled world while not expressing self-pity.

Many people will resist involvement with groups because to participate in a group would require them to have to "come out" in relation to two different aspects of their lives—one would be their handicap and the other would be their sexual orientation. In order to survive as a member of a minority or a member of minorities, most people use a great deal of denial: they may deny that they have a handicap, that their handicap limits them, that others treat them differently because of their handicap, that they feel differently because of their handicap, etc. In working with differently abled lesbian and gay men, it is important for the friend/counselor to respect the defenses that the differently abled person is using. After all, defenses may help all of us cope with the business of living our lives, which is sometimes more difficult than others. When the friend/counselor sees that the use of one's defenses is becoming inhibiting and limiting, that is the time to help the friend/client look at his/her behavior more carefully. For instance, denial could cause one to enter repeatedly into situations of rejection, to feel constantly injured, and not understand why. Denial could also cause them not to get adequate medical care, to be unaware of the fact that their disease is progressing, to "forget" about taking life-sustaining medication, etc.

Ricki Boden, a differently abled lesbian feminist therapist, has worked in groups with differently abled lesbians. In her work with these women, Ms. Boden found that, "Although it was not a linear progression, a process of Denial-Anger-Depression-Resolution emerged."[12] This process is very similar to what anyone who experiences a loss goes through (the reader may recall some of our discussion of this process in the chapter on AIDS in this book). It is an ongoing process. Many different situations can evoke the process: a much-dreaded doctor's appointment, a need for new braces, an increase in medication, diagnostic testing, etc. Painful experiences in different social situations may also evoke these responses: such as being the only single person in a group of couples, never having more than one date with someone, losing a lover and being afraid you will never find another, etc.

The knowledge that differently abled lesbians and gay men do go through the process of feeling denial, anger, depression, and resolution is especially important for the person interacting with differently abled people. This is because differently abled people often have accepted society's view of them as second-class citizens and have consequently repressed painful, often angry, feelings about how they have been treated or mistreated by the medical professions, their families, friends, and the general public. Since this may come on top of feeling second-class as a homosexual, they may be doubly oppressed and repressed! They may appear accepting of their inferior status when they really are in a rage. If the friend/counselor is aware that this can be so then he/she will be better able to listen to clues and explore such feelings. An example of this might be the following:

VINCENT. Sometimes I think it is a shame that I don't have a lover.

COUNSELOR. Why is that?

VINCENT. Well, I'm not really such a terrible person. I have a good sense of humor.

C. So?

VINCENT. Well, I really don't understand why my being in a

wheelchair creates so many problems. You'd think there was something wrong with me or something.

c. Do you think there is something wrong with you?

VINCENT. It's hard not to.

c. What do you mean?

VINCENT. Well, every time I go out with a new person, they never ask me out again. When I'm in a restaurant, they always put me by the door so as not to disturb the customers.

c. You sound discouraged.

VINCENT. Do I?

c. Yeah.

VINCENT. Well, maybe there is something wrong with me. It's hard seeing how many people don't want to be around me.

c. Is it just hard work?

VINCENT. Yeah.

c. Are you sure that's all?

VINCENT. Well, it's also very upsetting.

c. How is it upsetting?

VINCENT. It's upsetting because I can't blend in like everyone else does. There is always some sort of problem wherever I am or wherever I'm going.

c. You sound annoyed.

VINCENT. Who, me?

c. Yes, you.

VINCENT. It's funny because I don't think of myself as annoyed. Sometimes I think I'm mad . . . sometimes I resent everyone with two legs who can go wherever they want to go and then I feel bad 'cuz it's nobody's fault that I'm in this damn chair and the people with the good legs aren't.

c. Are you saying you feel guilty about feeling angry?

VINCENT. I never thought about it that way. Maybe you have a point. I guess I think I shouldn't be angry.

c. Why not?

VINCENT. They are not to blame that I'm in a wheelchair.

c. But that doesn't mean that you can't be angry because you are in one.

The friend/counselor in the above example did not accept Vince's being nice and accommodating. She clearly listened for what he was not saying and helped him bring it into consciousness.

In addition to the four clinical issues mentioned earlier, Boden also lists six additional issues for those working with differently abled persons to be aware of. They include:

1. Did the disability exist from birth or from an early age and did it have an adult onset?
2. Is the disability visible?
3. Race and class backgrounds produce different attitudes toward disability.
4. How much does the disability interfere with mobility?
5. What are the various levels of independence, dependence, and interdependence?
6. Is the disability fixed or progressive?[13]

As noted in our section on rural gays, the friend/counselor who is working with differently abled lesbians and gay men may find that it is necessary to do more outreach than we are used to, to do more basic education on what it means to be lesbian and gay (and sexual), and keep abreast of current information and resources that people can use in their exploration of their sexual orientation and their physical disability. One may have to do more telephone interviewing and/or home visits because distances can be so far and time and transportation less available. In addition, it is important that the friend/counselor be accessible and that he/she be able to meet with the friend/client in a barrier-free environment.

11

From the Present to the Future

On June 27, 1969, a police wagon pulled up in front of the Stonewall Inn in New York City. This was not unusual, since the police periodically raided the harassed patrons of gay and lesbian bars. The gay men and lesbians usually submitted peacefully. On the night of the twenty-seventh, however, the scenario did not proceed as usual. On that memorable night, the drag queens protested and bar customers resisted being taken away in police vehicles like criminals. This spontaneous protest represents what many consider to be the beginning of the gay rights movement. In 1970, New York City, Chicago, and Los Angeles held parades to commemorate the Stonewall Inn Riots. In 1972, San Francisco held its first official gay parade, "Christopher Street West." Although the initial people in the parades were lesbians and gay men, more and more heterosexuals participate every year to demonstrate their support for gay rights.

In working with lesbians and gay men, it is important to understand the place of civil rights in their lives. This means both those civil rights that do exist and those civil rights that do not exist. At the time of this writing only three states, Wisconsin, Massachusetts, and New Jersey, have civil rights statutes that protect lesbians and gay men. Twenty-five states and the District of Columbia still have sodomy laws that clearly give a message that there is something criminally wrong with being a homosexual. A few cities and states have specific legislation that protects housing and jobs. Tom Stoddard, the executive director of the Lambda Legal Defense and Education Fund, Inc.—America's oldest and largest legal organization dedicated to the rights of lesbian and gay men—estimates that only 10 percent of US lesbian and gay men are covered by legal protection in these areas (Kingston, New York, *Sunday Freeman*, June 25, 1989, p. 25).

Many people may have difficulty understanding and appreciating the important need for the current civil rights movement that lesbians and gay men are fighting in. The reality is that most homosexuals do not have equal protection under the law. A "straight" person usually does not lose a job because he/she is a heterosexual but a lesbian or gay man can lose his/her job because he/she is homosexual. Gay parents can lose their children because they are homosexual. Most lesbian and gay couples do not have legal rights as heterosexual married couples do: they are not allowed to file a joint tax return and they usually do not qualify for family insurance coverage. Gay people are not welcome in the military. They often are faced with security clearance problems. Homosexual aliens can be, and are, stopped at our borders. Some are returned to their country of origin. Others, with the help of such groups as Lambda, are allowed to stay.

What does this mean? The following excerpts from recent articles illustrate how these facts can impact on the real lives of gay men and lesbians:

> On December 29, 1988, Lambda filed a complaint in the Federal District Court for the District of Columbia charging the US Naval Academy with forcing Joseph Steffan, a highly commended midshipman, to resign less than one month before he was to graduate and receive a commission in the US Navy solely because he was gay. Mr. Steffan was in the top 10 percent of his class, was the premier soloist of the nationally renowned Glee Club and president of the Catholic choir. No sexual conduct was ever alleged by the Academy.[1]

> When Brian Forist tried to get a poster duplicated at the Pronto Printer copy store in Poughkeepsie's Main Mall, he thought there would be no trouble. The Ulster County Gay and Lesbian Alliance, for example, had printed material there. But after the poster was dropped off for reproduction, Forist received a message that there was a problem.
>
> When he spoke to the owner of the store, he was told to take his business elsewhere.
>
> "He said because of the nature of the work and the cause we're espousing he couldn't do the job," Forist said.

The poster, printed for last Friday's Heather Bishop Concert at McKenna Theater in SUNY New Paltz, included a line that read: "To Celebrate lesbian and gay pride."

Forist said he calmly told him that the reference to homosexuality "had never been printed so large; he had never noticed it (in the other printings)."

"This guy was real polite," Forist said, "He is a bigot, but he was a polite bigot."

The owner said he turned down the poster because of his Christian beliefs, not simply because Forist is gay. The phrase "To Celebrate lesbian and gay pride" offended him; and he chose not to reproduce such a statement.

"He (Forist) is asking me to separate myself as a person and as a businessman and I just can't do that. As a result, I just have a higher responsibility to the word of God vs. trying to make a dollar."

Not every Pronto Printer has a policy of refusing material related to gay and lesbian activities, Clark said, "each store is autonomous, pretty much." Each franchise must abide by rules, but Clark said the chain has no rule about matter related to gays and lesbians.[2]

Anglin v. Minneapolis Library Board (Minnesota)

Lambda represents a lesbian employee of the Minneapolis Library Board who has been refused the request to put her domestic partner of seven years on her health insurance policy. Jane Anglin asked to have her partner, Amy Goetz, added to the policy when Amy decided to go to law school. When the request was denied, Jane filed a grievance with her union, AFSCME, and a charge of discrimination with the Minneapolis Department of Civil Rights claiming discrimination based on marital status and affectional preference as prohibited by city law. Her employer, the Library Board, has been somewhat blocked in its efforts to provide a remedy by the City Attorney, who insists that the City should not provide benefits to "roommates. . . ."[3]

The title of a Forum sponsored by the American Conservative Union, "Gays and Their Rights: Should Either Exist?" A Bumper Sticker seen on the highways in California saying: "Kill a Queer for Christ."[4]

Morton Downey "Apologizes"

In an interview for airing April 27, television talk show host Morton Downey, Jr. backed away from the verbal gay-bashing that in part led to cancellation of his show in San Francisco. "I won't make a blanket indictment of any group ever again in my life," said Downey, who offered to tape television spots decrying violence towards gays. He said he has at least twenty gay friends with AIDS "who I will bury"—including his own brother.[5]

A nightmare: Sharon Kowalski, an active, vital Minnesota woman, is struck by a drunk driver, suffers brain damage, and is confined to a wheelchair. Even though she can communicate by typing, her father is appointed her guardian. He forbids her lover of four years to visit—the woman with whom she has taken lifetime vows and lived in their jointly owned home, and who is aiding her recovery by using physical therapy techniques. He denies that she is a lesbian, refuses to allow friends or lawyers to visit, and places her in a nursing home where she receives no rehabilitative care. She types, "Help me, Karen. Get me out of here. Please take me home with you." But this is Karen Thompson's last visit—she is barred from further contact by Minnesota court order. No one will tell Sharon that her lover is fighting for her freedom and her rights, or that "Free Sharon" committees have been formed across the nation.

This nightmare was two women's reality from November 1983 until recent months.

Last August 7, on Sharon Kowalski's thirty-second birthday, demonstrations took place in twenty-two cities throughout the country demanding that she be free. Subsequently, Sharon was tested for competency for the first time in the four years of her guardianship, even though the law requires annual testing. Following the competency report, Sharon was moved from the nursing home in which she had been incarcerated for almost four years to a rehabilitative facility in Duluth, Minnesota, and on February 2, 1989, Karen Thompson was finally allowed to visit. It was their first meeting since August 1985—a meeting which Karen and many others throughout the country had worked timelessly, fought, and prayed for.[6]

The above examples illustrate that, indeed, lesbians and gay men are the recipients of much discrimination. Not only are they discriminated against but they are also victims of a rising tide of antigay violence that takes place everywhere—in small towns, big cities, and rural areas. Some examples of gay violence include the following:

"I popped him in the mouth . . . . I'd put one gay in his place, but I was angry that he was gay and felt maybe like I should go back and just beat him up, but I had other things to do that day."[7]

The *New York Times,* August 24, 1989, reported that two men were attacked on the Upper West Side of Manhattan by a group of knife and bat wielding teenagers shouting anti-homosexual epithets. Mr. F. was stabbed twice in the back and suffered a collapsed lung. Mr. F. was treated for a possible fracture of his right elbow. . . . The number of assaults against people who are homosexual or are perceived by others to be homosexual has risen dramatically this year, said David Wertheimer, the Executive Director of the New York City Gay and Lesbian Anti Violence Project. The Project reports a 36% increase in violence against gays and lesbians in just the first 6 months of the year.[8]

In Pennsylvania last spring, a lone assailant stalked and shot two lesbians hiking in the mountains—killing one and seriously wounding the other. When police caught him, the attacker said he had been provoked because it was clear that the women were lesbian lovers.[9]

In Fort Wayne, Indiana, three teenagers with Chinese kung fu "throwing stars" invaded a gay bar and slashed three patrons.[10]

In rural North Carolina, members of the far-right "White Patriot Party" invaded a gay-oriented bookstore and shot five men— killing three. According to an informant, the murders were "to avenge Jehovah on homosexuals."[11]

Gay people aren't the only victims of anti-gay violence. In San Francisco, a heterosexual male tourist was stabbed to death by an assailant who first taunted him as a "faggot" and a "fruit."[12]

San Francisco's openly gay elected supervisor, Harvey Milk, and George Moscone were fatally shot by Supervisor Dan White on November 27, 1978. In 1985 *The Times of Harvey Milk* won the Oscar for best film documentary.

After reading the above examples, one might wonder why anyone would want to be lesbian or gay. The reality is that most lesbian and gay people do not choose their sexual orientation, just as most heterosexual people do not choose theirs. The only choice that lesbians and gay men have is that of deciding whether or not to practice or live out their sexual orientation. More and more people are making the choice not to deny who they are. Despite the fact that this is not a popular choice and that it makes one vulnerable to harassment, many people are choosing to come out to themselves and to others. As the poetess, Joan Larkin (1976) has described:

> Coming out, since it is no less than recognizing who I am and letting that be seen by others, is a source of strength and exhilaration. I used enormous amounts of energy hiding: now I can use that energy to meet my needs. I can do my work and give to my daughter, my lover, and others with the creativity released in me by self acceptance and self assurance.[13]

Lesbians and gay men have a long way to go, but some things are changing. The government has officially ended discrimination in civil service jobs. Twenty-five states have repealed their sodomy laws. The Human Rights Campaign Fund was named in 1988 as the ninth largest independent political action committee in the country. Lesbians and gay men are continually seeking legal action to fight for their rights.

In California, a federal court has issued the most definitive ruling yet, that:

> a Federal law barring discrimination against the handicapped protects healthy carriers of the AIDS virus as well as those who have actually developed the deadly disease.
>
> Earlier court cases had merely suggested that the law, the Federal Rehabilitation Act of 1973, applied to healthy carriers of the virus that causes acquired immune deficiency syndrome. The law prohibits institutions receiving Federal funds from discriminating against the handicapped."[14]

On May 1, 1989, the National Gay and Lesbian Task Force

launched the only national organizing project to secure recognition and protection for lesbian and gay families. Staffed by veteran feminist and black activist Ivy Young, the NGLTF "Lesbian and Gay Families Project" represents a unique collaboration between NGLTF and the San Francisco-based National Center for Lesbian Rights. . . . The Lesbian and Gay Families Project will educate, advocate and organize for full legal and societal recognition of lesbian and gay relationships and families.[15]

On July 16, 1989, the *New York Times* ran an article entitled, "T. W. A. Broadens Use of 'Frequent Flier' Tickets," which is significant for lesbians and gay men:

> Trans World Airlines has changed the policy of its "frequent flier" program in response to complaints and a lawsuit filed by a homosexual couple.
>
> Until recently, the airline required that people who earned free airline tickets by accumulating mileage on other trips use the free tickets themselves or have their relatives use them.
>
> Airline officials said the policy was intended to prevent people from selling or bartering the tickets. But gay men and lesbians complained that the policy was discriminatory because it did not permit them to share their free tickets with companions.
>
> "What we have now done is to expand the policy so that virtually any frequent flier can travel with any companion of their choosing," said Mark Buckstein, the airline's general counsel, "We felt our rules had probably been unduly restrictive."[16]

In late June 1989, the Hate Crimes Statistics Act passed the House of Representatives by an overwhelming vote. This was the first piece of prohomosexual legislation passed in the history of the US Congress. The purpose of this bill was to require the collection of statistics on crimes motivated by prejudice based on race, religion, homosexuality, heterosexuality or ethnicity. On February 8, 1990, the US Senate passed the bill by a landslide margin.

On July 7, 1989, the *New York Times* reported that New York State's highest court had expanded the legal definition of a family on July 6, 1989:

> holding that a gay couple who had lived together for a decade could be considered a family under New York City's rent control regulations. . . . In his majority opinion, Judge Vito J. Titone wrote that protection against eviction "should not rest on fictitious legal distinctions or genetic history, but instead could find its foundation in the reality of family life." "In the context of eviction," he added, "a more realistic, and certainly equally valid, view of a family includes two adult lifetime partners whose relationship

is long term and characterized by an emotional and financial commitment and interdependence."[17]

Some hospitals, such as Lenox Hill in New York City, state in their Patients Rights and Responsibilities pamphlets that patients cannot be discriminated against as to "race . . sexual orientation or source of payment." Change is happening—even if it is slow. There is an aura of hope.

Like everyone else, lesbians and gay men want to be free to enjoy their relationships, to have supportive friends, to have a family, to be able to have a career and a home. The fact that so many do is amazing when one considers how oppressive our society is and has been towards lesbians and gay men. Lesbians and gay men have had very few role models and little or no recorded history because homosexuals are not usually written about in textbooks or history books. Yet many talented homosexuals have made significant contributions to our culture. A partial list includes the following people: writer Henry James, journalist and lecturer Sabrina Sojourner, actor and dramatist Harvey Fierstein, politician Harvey Milk, writer Horatio Alger, Jr., playwright Lorraine Hansberry (A Raisin in the Sun), Singers Johnny Mathis, Janis Joplin, and Rod McKuen, writer Virginia Woolf, journalist Merle Miller, writer Oscar Wilde, and politician Harry Britt. Others include: writers Herman Melville and Kate Millet, composer Pyotr Ilich Tchaikovsky, poets Willa Cather and Amy Lowell, actor Charles Laughton, playwright Noël Coward, artist Andy Warhol, musician Benjamin Britten, tennis player Bill Tilden, actors Tyrone Power and Montgomery Clift, writer Carson McCullers, Truman Capote, Hart Crane, and May Sarton, as well as renowned theater personality Michael Bennett.

We are sharing this by no means complete list of notable lesbians and gay men to give you a more concrete idea of who some famous and well-known lesbians and gay men of recent times are. Some of you may be surprised by a few of the names we have mentioned. As we have noted, information that identifies lesbians and gay men of earlier times is not found in many text or history books. As a result of this fact, both heterosexuals and homosexuals are deprived of the opportunity to be able to identify with many wonderful and outstanding members of our society who are leaders in their own fields.

Lesbians and gay men have been around for a long time and have always produced leaders. And we always will, just as we will also continue to produce many special people who qualify as your "average citizen." It is the hope of the authors that our book has helped the reader to develop a better awareness and understanding of who lesbians and gay men are and of their various needs. It is also the hope of the authors that this book will help the reader become more sensitive to and aware of his/her negative feelings about lesbians and gay men. We all have prejudices. We are not always aware that they exist in us. We are also not always aware of the strength of their existence in us and the power and influence that they have in our lives and our interactions with other people. Prejudice comes from a lack of understanding and misunderstandings. It is our hope that this book will help our reader—the counselor/friend—dispel some of this misunderstanding and misinformation. Finally, it is the hope of the authors that this book will help the reader gain a greater appreciation of lesbians and gay men.

Appendix

Safer Sex

Safer sex practices are important for everyone—men and women; heterosexual, bisexual, and homosexual; teenagers; drug users; those who test HIV positive; those who have AIDS; etc. The safest way to prevent HIV infection and AIDS is to avoid all sexual interaction and the use of IV drugs. Abstinence is the only true form of prevention of AIDS. However, if you are sexual, and most people are, it is important to become familiar with the various aspects of safer sex practice. Since there really is no such thing as safe sex, the authors choose to use the term "safer sex," which refers to a series of precautions one can utilize to cut down on the risk of infection.

To begin with—know that you and your partner are not infected *by being tested* anonymously; have sex only with each other, and don't use IV drugs. Use a latex condom whenever you have oral, anal, or vaginal intercourse. When having anal or vaginal sex, the use of spermicide is also advised. The spermicide should contain nonoxynol-9, 4% or more strength, for most effectiveness. One should never use petroleum jelly with a condom. There are many sexual activities such as mutual masturbation, touching, fantasy, and massage that are pleasurable and usually do not involve contact with your partner's semen, blood, feces, or urine if practiced with a condom.

Lesbians tend to think that they are not at risk for the HIV virus. That is not true. Everyone is at risk. Some lesbians have had, or continue to have male sexual partners. Some lesbians and/or their partners have a history of drug abuse. Some 'lesbians' are closeted bi-sexuals. Lesbians on the whole do not

159

practice safer sex. Being a lesbian does not guarantee that a woman has not been with high risk people.

Lesbians need to participate in safer sex practices. When having oral sex, it is important to use a barrier such as a dental dam, a latex condom slit up the side, or even a heavy gauge household plastic wrap. No studies have been done on the use of these barriers but they are what we have available right now. Be sure to use a water based lubricant which contains nonoxynol-9. When using sex toys, it is important that they be sterilized after each use and that they not be passed back and forth between each partner. A condom can be used on a dildo for protection. Latex surgical gloves can also be used to protect your hand or finger(s).

Preventing AIDS is a mutual process. Honest, truthful communication is a key ingredient to this process. It is important to postpone sex until after you have a sense that you know and trust your partner. This is especially true because people often are not truthful or open about upsetting and anxiety producing topics such as sex and AIDS when they first meet. Interestingly enough, it is often easier for two people to be sexual rather than to talk about it. It can be very hard to withstand pressure from someone you are interested in. Just remember that it is your body and your life that you may be risking. You can always ask yourself why you need to agree to be sexual with someone who is not respecting your feelings or who does not seem very concerned about the need to be careful.

Glossary

Ageism	A bias against older people.
AIDS	Acquired immune deficiency syndrome. A disease that affects the immune system and makes one vulnerable to a wide range of opportunistic infections.
Bisexual	A person who establishes emotional and physical relationships with people of both genders.
Butch	Masculine behavior and/or physical appearance in a lesbian; supermasculine gay man.
Butch–Femme	Role playing by lesbian couples.
Coming out	A process by which one begins to think of one's self as lesbian or gay. It initially involves self-recognition and can move on to sharing one's lesbian or gay identity with others.
Dyke	A lesbian. Use of this word may imply a negative masculine connotation.
Faggot	A male homosexual.
Fairy	A gay man.
Femme	Feminine behavior and/or physical appearance in a lesbian.
Gay	Synonym for homosexual.
Heterosexual	Person attracted to people of the opposite sex.
HIV	Human immunodeficiency virus; the virus that causes AIDS.
HIV negative	Absence of the HIV antigens in the system.
HIV positive	Your body has been exposed to the virus.

161

Homophobia	Irrational fear and/or hatred of anyone or anything connected with homosexuality.
Homosexual	A person who is attracted to others of the same sex.
In the closet	Usually means keeping one's lesbian or gay identity a secret from friends, neighbors, business acquaintances, and/or family. Some people may be totally "in the closet" and others may be partially "in the closet."
Lesbian	A woman attracted socially, sexually, and emotionally to women.
Lezzie	A negative slang term for lesbian.
Life partner	Another term for lover.
Lover	The individual a lesbian or gay man couples with to meet his/her social, affectional, and sexual needs. They may or may not share a common living arrangement.
"Out"	Open about one's homosexuality. Not "in the closet."
Queen	An effeminate gay man.
Queer	A negative slang term for homosexual.
Significant other	Another term for lover.
Sodomy	Anal intercourse.
Straight	Synonym for heterosexual.

Notes

Chapter 2: What Do You Mean You Are Not Heterosexual?

1. A. Kinsey, W. Pomeroy, and C. Martin *Sexual Behavior in the Human Male* (Philadelphia: W. B. Saunders, 1953).
2. K. P. Johanns, "They Tried to 'Cure' Me of Lesbianism," in *Growing Up Gay* (Michigan: Youth Liberation Press, 1978), p. 37.
3. American Psychiatric Association, *Diagnostic and Statistical Manual of Mental Disorders*, Third Edition Revised (Washington, DC, 1989), pp. 168–69.

Chapter 3: Come Out, Come Out, Wherever You Are

1. V. Cass, "Homosexual Identity Formation: A Theoretical Model," *Journal of Homosexuality*, 4 (3), pp. 219–37.
2. J. Porcino, *Growing Older, Getting Better: A Handbook for Women in the Second Half of Life* (New York, NY: Continuum, 1991), pp. 192–93.
3. M. McDonald, "The Way We Were," *Lesbian Herstory Archives Newsletter*, 10, February 1988, p. 3.

Chapter 4: Religion

1. The Holy Bible: King James Version (New York: American Bible Association, 1987), p. 14.
2. Ibid., p. 690.
3. Ibid., p. 143.
4. Ibid., p. 193.
5. John J. McNeil, S. J., *The Church and the Homosexual* (Kansas City: Sheed, Andrews, & McMeel, Inc., 1976). pp. 41–42.
6. L. Scanzoni, and V. Mollenkott, *Is the Homosexual My Neighbor?* (San Francisco: Harper and Row, 1978), pp. 71–72.
7. John J. McNeil, p. 153.
8. *San Francisco Examiner,* June 18, 1989, p. A-12.
9. "Geraldo Rivera Show," Transcript 382, *Lesbian Teens and Their Mothers*, March 3, 1989.

164 | Notes

10. Lily Eng, "Bobby's Legacy," *San Francisco Examiner,* June 18, 1989, p. A-12.
11. *San Francisco Examiner,* June 18, 1989, p. A-12.
12. P. Moore, Jr., *Take a Bishop Like Me,* (New York: Harper and Row, 1979), pp. 112–15.

Chapter 5: Lesbian and Gay Youth

1. Aaron Fricke, *Reflections of a Rock Lobster, A Story About Growing up Gay* (Boston: Alyson Publications, Inc., 1981), pp. 7–8.
2. Geraldo Rivera Transcript 382, *Lesbian Teens and Their Mothers,* p. 1.
3. Anonymous, "Coming Out Carefully in Rural Michigan," *Growing Up Gay,* edited by K. Hefna and A. Sutin, (Michigan: Youth Liberation Press, 1978), p. 25.
4. Ibid., p. 26.
5. Lily Eng, "Bobby's Legacy," *San Francisco Examiner,* June 18, 1989, p. A-12.
6. "Dear Abby," *San Francisco Chronicle,* 1981.
7. Ibid., p. 26.
8. S. Freud (1935), "Letter to An American Mother" reprinted in Ronald Bayer, *Homosexuality and American Psychiatry* (Princeton: Princeton University Press, 1987), p. 27.

Chapter 6: Parenting

1. M. Shernoff and W. Scott, editors, *The Sourcebook on Lesbian and Gay Health Care* (Washington National Lesbian/Gay Health Foundation, 1988).
2. *Family Service America.* Information Packet. Milwaukee, WI, 1989.
3. G. Kolata, "Lesbian Partners Find the Means to be Parents," *New York Times,* January 30, 1989.
4. G. Schulenburg, *Gay Parenting* (Garden City, NY: Anchor Press/Doubleday, 1985).
5. *New York Times,* January 30, 1989.
6. *San Francisco Examiner,* June 12, 1989, p. A-18.
7. Ibid.
8. Petra Liljesfraud, "Children without Fathers: Handling the Anonymous Donor Question," *Outlook,* Fall 1988, pp. 25–29.

Chapter 7: AIDS: The Disease that Does Not Discriminate

1. C. E. Koop, "Understanding AIDS," (Maryland: HHS. Publication No. [COC] HHS, 88-8404), p. 2.
2. *"New York Native Reader* Profile," "The information herein contains the specific results of the readership survey mailed to 500 subscribers on October 21, 1988, and inserted into 2850 newstand copies distributed on October 23, 1988. The results are based upon a 62

percent response rate from subscribers and a 24.4 percent response rate from newstand copies, for a total of 679 completed questionnaires. All surveys were processed by Simmons Market Research Bureau, Inc., 380 Madison Avenue, New York, employing standard market research editing, coding, and tabulating procedures."

3. Cindy Ruskin, *The Quilt: Stories from The Names Project* (New York: Pocket Books, 1988).

Chapter 8: Older Lesbians and Gay Men

1. A. E. Moses and R. Hawkins, Jr., *Counseling Lesbian Women and Gay Men: A Life Issues Approach* (St. Louis: C. V. Mosby Company, 1982), p. 192.

2. M. Sarton, *Recovering: A Journal* (New York: W. W. Norton and Company, 1986), p. 10.

Chapter 9: Alcohol and Substance Abuse in the Lesbian and Gay Communities

1. "Alcohol Awareness" in *Our Voice* edited by K. Deniston, vol. 4, No. 1, March 1989, p. 1.

2. Barbara Faltz, "Substance Abuse and the Lesbian and Gay Community: Assessment & Intervention," *Sourcebook on Lesbian and Gay Health Care* (Washington: National Lesbian/Gay Health Foundation, 1988), p. 156.

3. G. DeSlefano, "Gay Drug Abuse," *The Advocate*, 449, June 24, 1986, pp. 42–47.

4. Ibid., p. 45.

Chapter 10: Special Need Groups within the Lesbian and Gay Communities

1. *San Francisco Examiner,* June 4, 1989, pp. B 3–4.

2. N. L. Wyers, "Homosexuality in the Family: Lesbian and Gay Spouses," *Social Work,* vol. 32, no. 2, March–April 1987, p. 144.

3. Ibid., p. 145.

4. F. Bozett, "Gay Fathers: Evolution of the Gay-Father Identity," *American Journal of Orthopsychiatry,* vol. 51, no. 3, July 1981, p. 554.

5. Wyers, p. 146.

6. Ibid.

7. E. Coleman, "Bisexual and Gay Men In Heterosexual Marriage: Conflicts and Resolutions in Therapy," *Homosexuality And Psychotherapy,* edited by J. Gonsiorek (New York: Haworth Press, 1982, Vol. 7, nos. 2–3), p. 102.

8. Paula Gunn Allen, "Beloved Women: The Lesbian In American Indian Culture," *Women-Identified Women,* edited by T. Darty and

Sandee Potter (Palo Alto, CA: Mayfield Publishing Company, 1984), p. 96.

9. Ibid., p. 86.
10. Vickie M. Mays and Susan Cochron, "The Black Women's Relationship Project: A National Survey of Black Lesbians," *The Source Book on Lesbian and Gay Health Care,* edited by M. Shernoff and W. Scott (Washington: National Gay and Lesbian Health Care Foundation, 1988), pp. 55–56.
11. E. Acosta, "Gay and Black in D.C.: "Emerging Dialogue Between Races," *The Blade,* Washington D.C., December 6, 1979, p. B5.
12. N. Rubin, "Clinical Issues with Disabled Lesbians: An Interview with Ricki Boden," *Catalyst: A Socialist Journal of the Social Services,* vol. 3, no. 4, 1981, p. 46.
13. Ibid., pp. 42–43.

Chapter 11: From the Present to the Future

1. "Docket Update," *Lambda Update,* Vol. 6, No. 4, Spring/Summer 1989, p. 9.
2. *Sunday Freeman,* Kingston, New York, June 25, 1989, p. 25.
3. "Docket Update," *Lambda Update,* Vol. 6, No. 4, Spring/Summer 1989, p. 9.
4. Promotional title from the Fund for Human Dignity
5. Newsletter, The Federation of Parents and Friends of Lesbians and Gays, Inc., No. 44, April–June 1989.
6. "Kowalski Up-Date", *Womenews,* June 1989, p. 5.
7. *San Francisco Examiner,* June 7, 1989, p. A-1.
8. *New York Times,* August 24, 1988, pp. B1 and B4.
9. Promotional Letter from the National Gay and Lesbian Task Force.
10. Ibid.
11. Ibid.
12. Ibid.
13. Joan Larkin, "Coming Out," *Ms. Magazine,* March 1976, p. 86.
14. Dennis Hevisi, "AIDS Carriers Win a Court Ruling," *New York Times,* July 9, 1988, p. 6.
15. "NGLTF Creates Families Project." *Task Force Report,* the NGLTE Newsletter, Spring, 1989, p. 1.
16. *New York Times,* July 16, 1989, p. 19.
17. *New York Times,* July 7, 1989, p. 1.

Bibliography and Reference List

AIDS

AIDS Education and Prevention, vol. 1, no. 1, Spring 1989, pp. 1 86.

Callen, Michael, editor. *The Newly Diagnosed,* published by the PWA Coalition, 263A West 19th Street, New York, NY 10011, 1987.

AIDS Information. Monthly bulletin of original papers published in biomedical journals. Swets Publishing Service, P.O. Box 825, 2160 SZ LISSE, Holland.

Berube, Allan. "Caught in the Storm: AIDS and the Meaning of Natural Disaster." *Outlook: National Lesbian and Gay Quarterly,* vol. 1, no. 3, Fall 1988, pp. 8–19.

Boland, Mary G., with Theodore J. Allen, Gwendolyn I. Long, and Mary Tasker. "Children with HIV Infection: Collaborative Responsibilities of the Child Welfare and Medical Communities." *Social Work,* November–December 1988, vol. 33, no. 6, pp. 504–9.

Chu, S., J. Buehler, P. Fleming, and R. Berkelman. "Epidemiology of Reported Cases of AIDS in Lesbians, United States 1980–89." *American Journal of Public Health,* November 1990, vol. 80, no. 11, pp. 1380–81.

Davidson, Rev. Robert. "AIDS is Not God's Wrath" (Sermon). October 20, 1985, West-Park Presbyterian Church, 165 West 86th Street, New York, NY 10024.

Galea, Robert P., Benjamin F. Lewis, and Lori A. Baker. "Voluntary Testing for HIV Antibodies among Clients in Long-Term Substance-Abuse Treatment." *Social Work,* May–June 1988, vol. 33, no. 3, pp. 265–68.

Gibson, Denise. "Women and HIV Disease: An Emerging Crisis," *Social Work,* January 1991, vol. 36, no. 1, pp. 22–27.

Gochros, Harvey I. "Risks of Abstinence: Sexual Decision Making in the AIDS Era," *Social Work,* May–June 1988, vol. 33, no. 3, pp. 254–56.

Haney, Patrick. "Providing Empowerment to the Person with AIDS." *Social Work,* May–June 1988, vol. 33, no. 3, pp. 251–53.

Hay, Louise L. *The AIDS Book: Creating a Positive Approach.* Santa Monica CA: Hay House, 1987.

"Helping People with AIDS." *Practice Digest,* Summer 1984, vol. 7, no. 1, pp. 23–25.

Hevisi, Dennis. "AIDS Carriers Win a Court Ruling." *New York Times,* July 9, 1988.

Huber, Jeffrey, editor. *How To Find Information About* AIDS, 2nd ed. New York: Harrington Park Press, 1992.

Kelly, James and Pamela Sykes. "Helping the Helpers: A Support Group for Family Members of Persons with AIDS." *Social Work,* May 1989, vol. 34, no. 3, pp. 239–42.

Koop, C. E., "Understanding AIDS." Maryland: HHS. Publication no. (COC) HHS—88-8404.

Krieger, Irwin. "An Approach to Coping with Anxiety about AIDS." *Social Work,* May–June 1988, vol. 33, no. 3, pp. 263–64.

Kübler-Ross, Elisabeth. *AIDS: The Ultimate Challenge.* New York: Macmillan Publishing Company, 1987.

Lester, Bonnie. *Women and AIDS: A Practical Guide for Those Who Help Others.* New York: Continuum Publishing Company, 1989.

Leonard, Zoe. "Lesbians in the AIDS Crisis." *Women, AIDS, and Activism,* edited by The Act Up/NY Women and AIDS Book Group. Boston: South End Press, 1990.

Lockhart, Lettie and John S. Wodarski. "Facing the Unknown: Children and Adolescents with AIDS," *Social Work,* May 1989, vol. 34, no. 3, pp. 215–21.

Lopez, Diego J. and George S. Getzel. "Helping Gay AIDS Patients in Crisis." *Social Casework: The Journal of Contemporary Social Work,* September 1984, pp. 387–94.

Martelli, Leonard J. with Fran D. Peltz, C. R. C. and William Messina, C.S.W. *When Someone You Know Has AIDS: A Practical Guide.* New York: Crown Publishers, 1987.

Miller, Jaclyn and Thomas O. Carlton. "Children and AIDS: A Need to Rethink Child Welfare Practice," *Social Work,* November–December 1988, vol. 33, no. 6, pp. 553–55.

Monette, Paul. *Borrowed Time: An Aids Memoir.* San Diego and New York: Harcourt, Brace, Jovanovich, 1988.

National Institute of Mental Health. *Coping With AIDS: Psychological and Social Considerations in Helping People with HTLV-III Infection.* A pamphlet sold by the Superintendent of Documents, US Government Printing Office, Washington, D.C. 20402, 1986.

The New York State Division of Women, The New York State Assembly Task Force on Women's Issues, The New York State Legislative Women's Caucus, and The Women and Aids Project. "Report of the Public Hearing on AIDS: Its Impact on Women, Children and Families, Summary of Testimony," June 12, 1987. A copy of this report can be obtained from the New York State Division for Women, State Executive Chamber, State Capitol, Albany, New York 12224.

Norwood, Chris. *Advice For Life: A Woman's Guide to AIDS Risks and Prevention.* New York: Pantheon Books, 1987.

Palacios-Jimenez, Luis and Michael Shernoff. *Facilitator's Guide to Eroticizing Safer Sex: A Psychoeducational Workshop Approach to Safer Sex Education.* New York: Gay Men's Health Crisis, 1986.

Pieters, Reverend Stephen A. "AIDS: A Christian Response." Published by the Universal Fellowship of Metropolitan Community Churches, 5300 Santa Monica Blvd., Suite 304, Los Angeles, CA.

Richardson, Diane. *Women and AIDS.* New York: Methuen, 1988.

Rounds, Kathleen A. "AIDS in Rural Areas: Challenges to Providing Care," *Social Work,* May–June 1988, vol. 33, no. 3, pp. 257–61.

Ruskin, Cindy. *The Quilt: Stories from the Names Project.* New York: Pocket Books, 1988.

Shilts, Randy. *And the Band Played On: Politics, People, and the AIDS Epidemic.* New York: St. Martin's Press, 1987.

Stulberg, Ian and Margaret Smith. "Psychosocial Impact of the AIDS Epidemic on the Lives of Gay Men." *Social Work,* May–June 1988, vol. 33, no. 3, pp. 277–81.

Tilleraas, Perry. *The Color of Light: Daily Meditations for All of Us Living with AIDS.* Center City, MN: Hazelden Foundation, 1988.

Treatment Issues: The GMHC Newsletter of Experimental AIDS Therapies. GMHC, Department of Medical Information, 129 West 20th Street, New York, NY 10011.

Washington HIV News, vol. 1, no. 3, August 1989, pp. 1–24.

Whitmore, George. *Someone Was Here: Profiles in the AIDS Epidemic.* New York: New American Library, 1989.

Adolescents

Back, Gloria Guss. *Are You Still My Mother? Are You Still My Family?* New York: Warner Books, 1985.

Bergstrom, Sage MSW and Lawrence Cruz, MSW, editors, *Counseling Lesbian and Gay Male Youth: Their Special Lives/Special Needs.* Washington, D.C.: The National Network of Runaway and Youth Services, Inc., 1983.

Brown, Rita Mae. *Rubyfruit Jungle.* New York: Daughters, 1973; New York: Bantam Books, 1977.

Fairchild, Betty and Nancy Hayword. *Now That You Know: What Every Parent Should Know About Homosexuality.* New York: Harcourt, Brace, Jovanovich, 1979.

Fricke, Aaron. *Reflections of a Rock Lobster: A Story About Growing Up Gay.* Boston: Alyson Publications, Inc., 1981.

Geraldo Rivera Show. "Lesbian Teens and Their Mothers." Transcript 382, March 3, 1989.

Hall, Lynn. *Sticks and Stones.* Chicago: Follett, 1972.

Hanckel, Frances and John Cunningham. *A Way of Love, A Way of Life: A Young Person's Introduction to What It Means to Be Gay.* New York: Lothan, Lee and Shepard Books, 1979.

Hefner, Keith and Al Sutin. *Growing Up Gay.* Ann Arbor: Youth Liberation Press, Inc. 1978.

Perry, Troy. *The Lord Is My Shepherd And He Knows I'm Gay.* University Fellowship M.C.C., 5300 Santa Monica Boulevard, Los Angeles, CA 90029, 1972.

Heron, Ann, editor. *One Teenager in 10: Writings by Gay And Lesbian Youth.* Boston: Alyson Publications, Inc., 1983.

Martin, Damien A. "Learning to Hide: The Socialization of the Gay Adolescent," *Adolescent Psychiatry: Developmental And Clinical Studies,* vol. 10, edited by Sherman C. Feinstein, John G. Looney, Allan Z. Schwartzberg, and Arthur D. Sorosky. Chicago: The University of Chicago, 1982, pp. 51–65.

Muller, Ann. *Parents Matter: Parents Relationships with Lesbian Daughters and Gay Sons.* Tallahassee, FL: Naiad Press, 1987.

Scoppettone, Sandra. *Happy Endings Are All Alike.* New York: Harper and Row, 1978.

Steinhorn, Audrey. "Lesbian Adolescents in Residential Treatment." *Social Casework,* October 1979, pp. 494–98.

Winterson, Jeannette. *Oranges Are Not the Only Fruit.* New York: Pandora Press, 1987.

White, Edmund. *A Boy's Own Story.* New York: The New American Library, 1983.

Family

"And Now, Gay Family Rights?" *Time,* December 13, 1982, p. 74.

Anonymous, Mary and Sarah. *Woman Controlled Conception.* n.p.: Womanshare Books, 1979.

Boston Lesbian Psychologies Collective, editors. "Lesbian Families: Psychosocial Stress and the Family Building Process," *Lesbian Psychologies.* Urbana, Illinois: University of Illinois Press, 1987.

Bozett, Frederick W. "Gay Fathers: Evolution of the Gay-Father Identity." *American Journal of Orthopsychiatry,* vol. 51, no. 3, July 1981, pp. 552–59.

Bozett, F., editor. *Gay and Lesbian Parents.* New York: Praeger, 1987.

Bradt, J. "Becoming Parents: Families With Young Children." *The Changing Family Life Cycle,* edited by Carter B. and McGoldrick. New York: Gardner, 1988.

Buxton, Amity. *The Other Side of the Closet: The Coming Out Crisis for Straight Spouses.* California: IBS Press, Inc., 1991.

Clunis, M. and D. Green. *Lesbian Couples.* Seattle: Seal Press, 1988.

Crawford, S. "Cultural Context as a Factor in the Expansion of

Therapeutic Conversation with Lesbian Families." *Journal of Strategic and Systemic Therapies*, vol. 7, no. 3, 1988.

Hall, Marny. "Lesbian Families: Cultural and Clinical Issues." *Social Work*, vol. 23, no. 5, September 1978, pp. 380–85.

Family Service of America. Information Packet. Milwaukee, WI, 1989.

Francoeur, Robert T. PhD, ACS. "Reproductive Techniques: New Alternatives And New Ethics." *Siecus Report*, vol. 14, no. 1, September 1985, ISSN O091-3995, pp. 1–5.

Gibson, Clifford Guy with the cooperation of Mary Jo Risher. *By Her Own Admission: A Lesbian Mother's Fight to Keep Her Son*. New York: Doubleday, 1977.

Goohros, Harvey L. "Gay Husbands." *Journal of Sex Educators and Therapists*, January 1978.

Goldstein, Richard. "The Bond That Dare Not Speak Its Name: Gay Life 1986." *The Village Voice*, July 1, 1986.

Green, Richard. "Sexual Identity of 37 Children Raised by Homosexual or Transexual Parents." *American Journal of Psychiatry*, vol. 135, no. 6, June 1978, p. 696.

Gutis, Philip S. "What Is a Family? Traditional Limits Are Being Redrawn." *New York Times*, August 31, 1989, pp. C1, C6.

Harry, Joseph, PhD. "Decision Making and Age Differences Among Gay Male Couples." *Journal of Homosexuality*, Winter 1982, vol. 8, no. 2, pp. 9–21.

Hitchens, Donna J., J.D. and Ann G. Thomas, Ed.D, editors. *Lesbian Mothers And Their Children: An Annotated Bibliography Of Legal And Psychological Materials*, San Francisco: Lesbian Rights Project, 1980.

Hoeffer, Beverly. "Children's Acquisition of Sex-Role Behavior in Lesbian–Mother Families." *American Journal of Orthopsychiatry*, vol. 51, no. 3, July 1981, pp. 536–44.

Kirkpatrick, Martha, Catherine Smith, and Ron Roy. "Lesbian Mothers and Their Children: A Comparative Survey." *American Journal of Orthopsychiatry*, vol. 51, no. 3, July 1981, pp. 545–51.

Levy, E. "Lesbian Motherhoods Identity and Social Support." *Affilia*, vol. 4, no. 4, 1989.

Liljesfraund, Petra. "Children without Fathers: Handling the Anonymous Donor Question." *Outlook: National Lesbian and Gay Quarterly*, vol. 1, no. 3, Fall 1988, pp. 24–29.

Maddox, Brenda. "Homosexual Parents." *Psychology Today*, February 1982, pp. 62–69.

MacPike, Loralee, editor. *There's Something I've Been Meaning To Tell You.* Tallahassee, FL: Naiad Press, 1989.

Marcus, Eric. *The Male Couple's Guide to Living Together.* New York: Harper and Row, 1988.

Martin, A. "Lesbian Parenting," *Gender in Transition*, edited by Joan Offerman-Zuckerbey. New York: Plenum, 1989.

McWhirter, David P. MD and Andrew Mattison MSW, PhD. "Psycho-therapy for Gay Male Couples." *A Guide to Psychotherapy with Gay and Lesbian Clients,* edited by John C. Gonsiorek. New York: Harrington Park Press, 1985, pp. 79–91.

———. *The Male Couple: How Relationships Develop.* Englewood Cliffs, NJ: Prentice-Hall, 1984.

———. "Treatment of Sexual Dysfunction in Homosexual Male Cou-ples." S. R. Leiblum and L. A. Pervin, editors, *Principles and Practices of Sex Therapy.* New York: Guilford Press, 1980.

Newsletter. Denver: Federation of Parents and Friends of Lesbians and Gays, no. 44, April–June 1989.

"NGLTF Creates Families Project." *Task Force Report.* Washington, DC: National Gay and Lesbian Task Force, Spring 1989.

Pies, Cheri. *Considering Parenthood: A Workbook for Lesbians.* San Fran-cisco: Spinsters Ink, 1985.

Pollach, Sandra and Jeanne Vaughn, editors. *Politics of the Heart: A Lesbian Parenting Anthology.* Ithaca, New York: Firebrand Books, 1987.

Rafkin, Louise. *Different Daughters: A Book by Mothers of Lesbians.* Pitts-burgh and San Francisco: Cleis Press, 1987.

Rafkin, Louise, editor. *Different Mothers: Sons and Daughters of Lesbians Talk About Their Lives.* San Francisco: Cleis Press, 1990.

Riddle, D. "Relating to Children: Gays As Role Models." *Journal of Social Issues,* vol. 34, no. 3, 1978, pp. 38–58.

Severance, Jane. *When Megan Went Away.* Chapel Hill, N.C.: Lollipop Power, Inc., 1979.

Schulenberg, J. *Gay Parenting: A Complete Guide for Gay Men and Lesbians with Children.* New York: Anchor Press, 1985.

Steinhorn, Audrey I. "Lesbian Mothers—The Invisible Minority: Role Of The Mental Health Worker." *Women and Therapy,* vol. 1, no. 4, pp. 35–48.

———. "Lesbian Adolescents In Residential Treatment," *Social Case-work,* vol. 60, no. 3, pp. 494–98.

——— and Helen McDonald CSW. "Lesbian and Gay Parents." *The Sourcebook On Lesbian/Gay Health Care,* second edition, edited by Michael Shernoff, MSW, ACSW and William A. Scott, MSW, ACP. Washington, DC: National Lesbian/Gay Health Foundation, 1988, pp. 246–49.

Walters, M. et. al. *The Invisible Web.* New York: Guilford Press, 1988.

Tanner, Donna M. *The Lesbian Couple,* Lexington, MA: D. C. Heath and Company, 1978.

Tessina, Tina, PhD. *Gay Relationships: How to Find Them, How to Improve Them, How to Make Them Last.* Los Angeles: Jeremy P. Tarcher, 1989.

Wyers, Norman L. "Homosexuality in the Family: Lesbian and Gay Spouses." *Social Work,* vol. 32, no. 2, March–April 1987, pp. 143–48.

General

American Psychiatric Association. *Diagnostic and Statistical Manual of Mental Disorders,* third edition, revised. Washington, DC, 1989.

Baetz, Ruth. "The Coming-Out Process: Violence against Lesbians." *Women-Identified Women,* edited by Trudy Darty and Sandee Potter. Palo Alto, CA: Mayfield Publishing Company, 1984, pp. 45–50.

Bell, Alan P., Martin S. Weinberg, and Sue Kiefer Hammersmith. *Sexual Preference: Its Development in Men and Women.* Bloomington: Indiana University Press, 1981.

Berzon, Betty, PhD. *Permanent Partners.* New York: E. P. Dutton, 1988.

———. *Positively Gay.* Los Angeles: Mediamix Associates, 1984.

Blumfield, Warner J. and Diane Raymond. *Looking At Gay And Lesbian Life.* Boston: Beacon Press, 1989.

Burger, Raymond Mark. "An Advocate Model for Intervention with Homosexuals." *Social Work,* July 1977, vol. 22, no. 4, pp. 280–83.

Borhek, M. V. *Coming Out To Parents; A Two-Way Survival Guide for Lesbians and Gay Men and Their Parents.* New York: Pilgrim Press, 1983.

Carrera, Michael. "Bisexuality." *Sex: The Facts, The Acts and Your Feelings.* New York: Crown Publishers, 1981, pp. 186–92.

———. "Homosexuality." *Sex: The Facts, The Acts and Your Feelings.* New York: Crown Publishers, 1981, pp. 163–85.

Cass, V. "Homosexual Identity Formation: A Theoretical Model." *Journal of Homosexuality,* vol. 4, no. 3, pp. 219–37.

Clark, Don. *As We Are.* Boston: Alyson Publications, 1988.

———. *Loving Someone Gay.* Bergenfield, NJ: New American Library, 1978.

———. *The New Loving Someone Gay.* Berkeley, CA: Celestial Arts, 1987.

"Dear Abby." *San Francisco Chronicle,* 1981.

DeCecco, John P., editor. "Bisexual And Homosexual Identities: Critical Clinical Issues." *Journal of Homosexuality,* vol. 9, no. 4, 1984.

———, editor. "Controversy Over the Bisexual and Homosexual Identities: Commentaries and Reactions." *Journal of Homosexuality,* Winter 1984, vol. 10, nos. 3–4, pp. 1–172.

———, editor. "Gay Relationships." *Journal of Sex Education and Therapy,* vol. 14, no. 2, Fall/Winter 1988.

"Docket Update." *Lambda Update,* vol. 6, no. 4, Spring/Summer 1989.

Dulaney, Diana D. and James Kelly. "Improving Services to Gay and Lesbian Clients." *Social Work,* vol. 27, no. 2, March 1982, pp. 178–83.

Freedman, Mark. "Homosexuals May Be Healthier than Straights." *Psychology Today,* vol. 81, no. 10, March 1975, p. 28.

Freud, Sigmund (1935). "Letter to An American Mother." Reprinted in Ronald Bayer, *Homosexuality and American Psychiatry.* Princeton: Princeton University Press, 1987.

Gonsiorek, John C., editor. *A Guide to Psychotherapy with Gay and Lesbian Clients.* New York: Harrington Park Press, 1985.

————. "Homosexuality and Psychotherapy." *Journal of Homosexuality,* vol. 7, nos. 2–3, Winter/Spring 1981-82, pp. 1–208.

Green, Richard MD. *Sexual Identity Conflict in Children and Adults.* Baltimore: Penguin Books, 1975.

Hayden, Curry and Denis Clifford. *A Legal Guide for Lesbian and Gay Couples.* Berkeley: Nolo Press, 1989.

Hidalgo, Hilda, Travis L. Peterson, and Natalie Jane Woodman, editors. *Lesbian and Gay Issues: A Resource Manual for Social Workers.* Silver Spring, MD: National Association of Social Workers, 1985.

Jones, Clinton R. *Understanding Gay Relatives and Friends.* New York: Seabury Press, 1978.

Kingston Sunday Freeman, June 25, 1989.

Kwawer, Jay S. PhD. "Transference and Countertransference in Homosexuality—Changing Psychoanalytic Views." *American Journal of Psychotherapy,* vol. 34, no. 1, January 1980, pp. 72–79.

Klein, Charna. *Counseling Our Own: The Lesbian/Gay Subculture Meets the Mental Health System.* Renton, WA: Publication Service, 1986.

Klein, Fritz, MD and Timothy J. Wolf. "Bisexualities: Theory and Research." *Journal of Homosexuality,* Spring 1985, vol. 11, nos. 1–2, pp. 1–232.

"Kowalski Up-Date." *Womenews,* June 1989.

Larkin, Joan. "Coming Out." *Ms.,* March 1976.

Marmor, Judd, editor. *Homosexual Behavior: A Modern Reappraisal.* New York: Basic Books, 1980.

Marotta, Toby. *The Politics of Homosexuality.* Boston: Houghton Mifflin, 1981.

Miller, Neil. *In Search of Gay America,* New York: The Atlantic Monthly Press, 1989.

Moses, A. Elfin and Robert O. Hawkins, Jr. *Counseling Lesbian Women and Gay Men: A Life Issues Approach.* St. Louis: C. V. Mosby Company, 1982.

New York Times, August 24, 1988.

————, July 7, 1989.

————, July 16, 1989.

"New York Native Reader Profile." Simmons Market Research Bureau, Inc., 380 Madison Avenue, New York, NY, October 1988.

Peplau, Letitia Anne, PhD and Randall W. Jones, MA, guest editors. "Symposium on Couples," *Journal of Homosexuality,* Winter 1982, vol. 8, no. 2, pp. 1–89.

"Psychology and the Gay Community." *Journal of Social Issues,* vol. 34, no. 3, 1978, pp. 1–142.

Rabin, Jack, Kathleen Keefe, and Michael Burton. "Enhancing Services for Sexual-Minority Clients: A Community Health Approach." *Social Work,* July–August, 1986, vol. 31, no. 4, pp. 294–98.

Reid, John. *The Best Little Boy in the World.* New York: Putnam, 1973.

Reiter, Laura. "Sexual Orientation, Sexual Identity, and the Question of Choice." *Clinical Social Work Journal,* Summer 1989, vol. 17, no. 2, pp. 138–50.

"Removing The Stigma." Final Report of the Board of Social and Ethical Responsibility for Psychology's Task Force on the Status of Lesbian and Gay Male Psychologists, Washington, D.C.: American Psychological Association, September, 1979.

Rivera, Rhonda R. "Our Straight-Laced Judges: The Legal Position of Homosexual Persons in the United States," *Hastings Law Journal,* vol. 30, no. 4, March 1979, pp. 799–955.

Ross, Michael W., guest editor. "Psychopathology and Psychotherapy in Homosexuality." *Journal of Homosexuality,* 1988, vol. 15, nos. 1–2, pp. 1–210.

Scanzoni, L. and V. Mollenkott. *Is the Homosexual My Neighbor?* San Francisco: Harper and Row, 1978.

Shernoff, Michael MSW, ACSW and William A. Scott, MSW, ACP, editors. *The Sourcebook On Lesbian/Gay Health Care, second edition.* Washington, DC: National Lesbian/Gay Health Foundation, 1988.

———. "Integrating Safer-Sex Counseling Into Social Work Practice." *Social Casework,* 1988.

Silverstein, Dr. Charles. *A Family Matter: A Parent's Guide to Homosexuality.* New York: McGraw-Hill, 1978.

"Symposium: Sexual Preference and Gender Identity." *Hastings Law Journal,* March 1979, vol. 30, no. 4.

Wilson, Lawrence A., and Raphael Shannon. "Homosexual Organizations and the Right of Association." *Hastings Law Journal,* vol. 30, no. 4, March 1979, pp. 1029–74.

"Working with Gay and Lesbian Clients." *Practice Digest,* vol. 7, no. 1, Summer 1984, pp. 3–31.

History

Berube, Allan. *Coming Out Under Fire: The History of Gay Men and Women in World War II.* New York: The Free Press, 1990.

Brown, H. *Familiar Faces, Hidden Lives.* New York: Harcourt, Brace, Jovanovich, 1976.

Cowan, Thomas. *Gay Men and Women Who Enriched The World.* New Canaan, CT: Mulvey Books, 1988.

Duberman, Martin, Vicinus, Martha, and George Chauncey, Jr., editors. *Hidden From History: Reclaiming The Gay And Lesbian Past.* New York: New American Library, 1989.

"Gay In America." *San Francisco Examiner,* June 4, 1989–June 17, 1989.

Hooker, Evelyn. "Homosexuality." *International Encyclopedia of the Social Sciences,* vol. 14. New York: Macmillan and Co., 1968, pp. 222–32.

Katz, Jonathan. *Gay American History: Lesbians and Gay Men in the USA.* New York: Thomas Y. Crowell Company, 1976.

Umans, Meg, editor. *Like Coming Home: Coming Out Letters.* Austin: Banned Books. 1988.

Russo, Vito. *The Celluloid Closet.* New York: Harper and Row. 1981.

Lesbians and Bisexual Women

Aldrich, Ann. *Take A Lesbian to Lunch.* New York: Macfadden Bartell Corporation, 1972.

Anthony, Bronwyn D. PhD. "Lesbian Client–Lesbian Therapist: Opportunities and Challenges in Working Together." *A Guide to Psychotherapy with Gay and Lesbian Clients,* edited by John C. Gonsiorek. New York: Harrington Park Press, 1985, pp. 45–57.

"A Bereavement Group for Lesbians." *Practice Digest,* Summer 1984, vol. 7, no. 1, p. 27.

Baetz, Ruth. *Lesbian Crossroads.* Tallahassee, FL: Naiad Press, 1988.

Beck, Evelyn Torton, editor. *Nice Jewish Girls: A Lesbian Anthology,* Watertown, MA: Persephone Press, 1982.

Becker, Carol. *Unbroken Ties: Lesbian Ex-Lovers.* Boston: Alyson Publications, 1988.

Boston Lesbian Psychologies Collective, editors. *Lesbian Psychologies: Explorations and Challenges.* Urbana: University of Illinois Press, 1987.

Bradford, Judith and Ryan Caitlin. *The National Lesbian Health Care Survey Final Report.* Washington, DC: National Lesbian/Gay Health Foundation, 1988.

Brown, Rita Mae. *Songs to a Handsome Woman.* Baltimore: Diana Press, 1973.

Califia, Pat, editor. *The Lesbian S/M Safety Manual.* San Francisco: Lace Publications, 1988.

———. *Sapphistry: The Book of Lesbian Sexuality,* Tallahassee. FL: Naiad Press, 1983.

Cruikshank, Margaret, editor. *The Lesbian Path.* Tallahassee, FL: Naiad Press, 1981.

Darty, Trudy and Sandee Potter, editors. *Women-Identified Women,* Palo Alto, CA: Mayfield Publishing Company, 1984.

Dykewoman, Elana, editor. *Sinister Wisdom.* Fall 1987, vol. 33.

Eisenbud, Ruth Jean. "Early and Later Determinants of Lesbian Choice." *The Psychoanalytic Review.* Spring 1982, vol. 69, no. 1, pp. 85–109.

Faberman, Lillian, PhD. "The New Gay Lesbians," *The Journal of Homosexuality,* Winter 1984, vol. 10, nos. 3–4, pp. 85–95.

———. *Odd Girls and Twilight Lovers: A History of Lesbian Life in 20th Century America.* New York: Columbia University Press, 1991.

Fuss, Diana, editor. *Inside/Out: Lesbian Theories, Gay Theories.* New York: Routledge, 1991.

Galana, Laurel and Gina Civina. *The New Lesbians: Interviews with Women Across the US and Canada.* San Francisco: Moon Books, 1977.

Gonsiorek, John C., Ph.D., editor. "Homosexuality and Psychotherapy: A Practitioner's Handbook of Affirmative Models." *Journal of Homosexuality,* Winter/Spring 1981/82, vol. 7, nos. 2–3, pp. 9–208.

Goodman, Bernice. *The Lesbian: A Celebration of Difference.* Brooklyn, NY: Out Books, 1977.

Grier, Barbara. *The Lesbian in Literature.* Tallahassee, FL: Naiad Press, 1981.

Hall, Radcliff. *The Well of Loneliness.* New York: Covici-Friede, 1929.

Hutchins, Loraine and Lani Kaahumanu. *Bi Any Other Name: Bisexual People Speak Out.* Boston: Alyson Publications, 1991.

Johnston, Jill. *Lesbian Nation: The Feminist Solution.* New York: Simon and Schuster, 1973.

Kirkpatrick, Martha and Carol Morgan. "Psychodynamic Psychotherapy of Female Homosexuality," *Homosexual Behavior: A Modern Reappraisal,* edited by Judd Marmor. New York: Basic Books, 1980, pp. 357–76.

Klaich, Delores. *Woman and Woman: Attitudes Toward Lesbianism.* New York: William Morrow, 1975.

Klein, Charna. *Counseling Our Own: The Lesbian/Gay Subculture Meets the Mental Health System.* Renton, WA: Publication Service, 1986.

Lewis, Lou Ann. "The Coming-Out Process for Lesbians: Integrating a Stable Identity." *Social Work,* September/October 1984, vol. 29, no. 5, pp. 464–69.

Lewis, Sasha Gregory. *Sunday's Women: A Report on Lesbian Life Today,* Boston: Beacon Press, 1979.

Lobel, Kerry, editor. *Naming the Violence: Speaking Out about Lesbian Battering.* Seattle: Seal Press, 1986.

Loulan, JoAnn. *Lesbian Sex.* San Francisco: Spinsters/aunt lute, 1984.

McDonald, M. "The Way We Were." *Lesbian Herstory Archives Newsletter,* no. 10, February 1988.

Maggiore, Dolores J. *Lesbianism: An Annotated Bibliography and Guide to the Literature, 1976–1986,* Metuchen, NJ and London: The Scarecrow Press, Inc. 1988.

Miller, Isabel. *Patience and Sarah.* Greenwich, CT: Fawcett Publications, 1973.

Myron, Nancy and Charlotte Bunch, editors. *Lesbianism and the Women's Movement,* Baltimore: Diana Press Publications, 1975.

Peplau, Letitia Anne, PhD, Christine Padesky PhD, and Mykol Hamilton MA. "Satisfaction in Lesbian Relationships." *Journal of Homosexuality,* Winter 1982, vol. 8, no. 2, pp. 23–35.

Ponse, Barbara. "Lesbians and Their Worlds." *Homosexual Behavior: A*

Modern Reappraisal, edited by Judd Marmor. New York: Basic Books, 1980, pp. 157–75.

Potter, Sandra J. and Trudy E. Darty. "Social Work and the Invisible Minority: An Exploration of Lesbianism." *Social Work,* May 1981, vol. 26, no. 3, pp. 187–92.

Rab Roth, Sallyann. "Psychotherapy with Lesbian Couples: Individual Issues, Female Socialization, and the Social Context." *Journal of Marital and Family Therapy,* 1985, vol. 11, no. 3, pp. 273–86.

Rothblum, Esther D. and Ellen Cole, editors. *Loving-Boldly: Issues Facing Lesbians,* New York: Harrington Park Press, 1989.

Saghir, Marcel T. and Eli Robins. "Clinical Aspects of Female Homosexuality." *Homosexual Behavior; A Modern Reappraisal,* edited by Judd Marmor. New York: Basic Books, 1980, pp. 280–95.

Samois, Members of. *Coming to Power: Writings and Graphics on Lesbian S/M.* Boston: Alyson Publications, 1982.

Sausser, Gail. *Lesbian Etiquette.* Trumansburg, NY: The Crossing Press, 1986.

Silveira, Jeanette, editor. *Lesbian Ethics,* Spring, 1985, vol. 1, no. 2.

Simpson, Ruth. *From the Closet to the Courts: The Lesbian Transition.* New York: Penguin Books, 1977.

Sisley, Emily Dr. and Bertha Harris, editors. *The Joy of Lesbian Sex,* New York: Crown Publishers, 1977.

The Nomadic Sisters. *Loving Women,* Sonora, CA: The Nomadic Sisters, 1975.

"The Lesbian Issue." *Resources for Feminist Research/Documentation Sur la Recherche Feministe,* vol. 12, no. 1, March 1983, pp. 1–110.

"Therapeutic Issues With Lesbian Clients." *Women and Therapy: A Feminist Quarterly,* vol. 1, no. 4, 1982, pp. 27–83.

Vetere, Victoria A. MSW. "The Role of Friendship in the Development and Maintenance of Lesbian Love Relationships." *Journal of Homosexuality,* Winter 1982, vol. 8, no. 2, pp. 51–65.

Wolfe, Susan J. and Julia Penelope Stanley, editors. *The Coming Out Stories,* Watertown, MA: Persephone Press, 1980.

Wolff, Charlotte, MD. *Love Between Women,* New York: Harper and Row, 1972.

Women's Resources, editor. *Considerations in Therapy with Lesbian Clients.* Philadelphia: Omega Press, 1979.

Gay and Bisexual Men

Anderson, Craig L., MSW. "Males As Sexual Assault Victims: Multiple Levels of Trauma." *Journal of Homosexuality,* Winter/Spring, 1981/1982, vol. 7, nos. 2–3, pp. 145–62.

Brown, Howard, MD. *Familiar Faces Hidden Lives: The Story of Homosexual Men in America Today.* New York: Harcourt, Brace, Jovanovich, 1976.

Coleman, Eli, PhD. "Bisexual and Gay Men in Heterosexual Marriage: Conflicts and Resolutions in Therapy." *A Guide to Psychotherapy with Gay and Lesbian Clients*, edited by John C. Gonsiorek. New York: Harrington Park Press, 1985, pp. 93–103.

Conlin, David, MSW and Jaime Smith, MD. "Group Psychotherapy for Gay Men." *A Guide to Psychotherapy with Gay and Lesbian Clients*, edited by John C. Gonsiorek. New York: Harrington Park Press, 1985, pp. 105–12.

Friedman, Richard. *Male Homosexuality: A Contemporary Psychoanalytic Perspective.* New Haven: Yale University Press, 1988.

Gochros, Jean Schaar, PhD. *When Husbands Come Out of the Closet.* New York: Harrington Park Press, 1989.

Hetrick, Emery and Terry Stein. *Innovations in Psychotherapy with Homosexuals*, Washington, DC: American Psychiatric Press, 1984.

Hobson, Laura Z. *Consenting Adult.* Garden City, NY: Doubleday and Company, 1975.

Isay, Richard A. MD. *Being Homosexual: Gay Men And Their Development.* New York: Farrar, Straus, and Giroux, 1989.

Kinsey, A., W. Pomeroy, and C. Martin. *Sexual Behavior in the Human Male.* Philadelphia: W. B. Saunders, 1953.

Levine, Martin P., editor. *Gay Men: The Sociology of Male Homosexuality.* New York: Harper and Row, 1979.

Lewis, Kenneth. *The Psychoanalytic Theory of Male Homosexuality.* New York: Simon and Schuster, 1988.

Malyon, Alan K., PhD. "Psychotherapeutic Implications of Internalized Homophobia in Gay Men." *A Guide to Psychotherapy with Gay and Lesbian Clients*, edited by John C. Gonsiorek. New York: Harrington Park Press, 1985, pp. 59–69.

Marmor, Judd. "Clinical Aspects of Male Homosexuality." *Homosexual Behavior: A Modern Reappraisal*, edited by Judd Marmor. New York: Basic Books, 1980, pp. 267–79.

Myers, Michael F., MD. "Counseling the Parents of Young Homosexual Male Patients." *Journal of Homosexuality*, Winter/Spring, 1981/1982, vol. 7, nos. 2–3, pp. 131–43.

Ostro, D. G. and T. A. Sandholtzer and Y. M. Felman. *Sexually Transmitted Diseases in Homosexual Men.* New York: Plenum, 1983.

Ovesey, Lionel and Sherwyn M. Woods. "Pseudohomosexuality and Homosexuality in Men: Psychodynamics as a Guide to Treatment." *Homosexual Behavior: A Modern Reappraisal*, edited by Judd Marmor. New York: Basic Books, 1980, pp. 325–41.

Reece, Rex, PhD. "Special Issues in the Etiologies and Treatments of Sexual Problems Among Gay Men." *Journal of Homosexuality*, edited by Michael W. Ross, 1988, vol. 15, nos. 1–2, pp. 43–57.

Rinsler, C. "The Return of the Condom." *American Health*, July 1987.

Sanders, David S., "A Psychotherapeutic Approach to Homosexual

Men." *Homosexual Behavior: A Modern Reappraisal,* edited by Judd Marmor. New York: Basic Books, 1980, pp. 342–56.

Sprague, Gregory A., PhD. "Male Homosexuality in Western Culture: The Dilemma of Identity and Subculture in Historical Research." *Journal of Homosexuality,* Winter 1984, vol. 10, nos. 3–4, pp. 29–43.

Walker, Mitch. *Men Loving Men: A Gay Sex Guide and Consciousness Book.* San Francisco: Gay Sunshine Press, 1977.

White, Edmund. *The Beautiful Room is Empty.* New York: Alfred A. Knopf, 1988.

Minorities

Acosta, E. "Gay and Black in DC: Emerging Dialogue Between Races." *The Blade,* December 6, 1979.

Allen, Paula Gunn. "Beloved Women: The Lesbian in American Indian Culture." *Women-Identified Women,* edited by Trudy Darty and Sandee Potter. Palo Alto, CA: Mayfield Publishing Company, 1984, pp. 83–96.

Brant, Beth. "Reclamation: A Lesbian Indian Story." *Women-Identified Women,* edited by Trudy Darty and Sandee Potter. Palo Alto, CA: Mayfield Publishing Company, 1984, pp. 97–103.

Corwell, Anita, *Black Lesbian in White America.* Tallahassee, FL: Naiad Press, 1983.

Hidalgo, Hilda. "The Puerto Rican Lesbian in the United States." *Women-Identified Women,* edited by Trudy Darty and Sandee Potter. Palo Alto, CA: Mayfield Publishing Company, 1984, pp. 83–96.

——— and Christensen, Elia Hidalgo. "The Puerto Rican Lesbian and the Puerto Rican Community." *Journal of Homosexuality,* vol. 2, no. 3, 1976, pp. 109–21.

Mullings, Keith. "Critique: Racism, Group Identity, and Mental Health." *International Journal of Mental Health,* vol. 7, nos. 3–4, 1979.

Ramos, Juanita, editor. *Companeras: Latina Lesbians (An Anthology).* New York: Latina Lesbian History Project, 1987.

Roberts, J.R., compiler. *Black Lesbians,* Tallahassee, FL: Naiad Press, 1981.

Roscoe, Will, coordinating editor. *Living the Spirit: A Gay American Indian Anthology (Compiled by Gay American Indians).* New York: St. Martin's Press, 1988.

Rubin, N. "Clinical Issues with Disabled Lesbians: An Interview with Ricki Boden." *Catalyst: A Socialist Journal of the Social Services,* vol. 3, no. 4, 1981.

Shockley, Ann Allen. "The Black Lesbian in American Literature: An Overview." *Women-Identified Women,* edited by Trudy Darty and Sandee Potter. Palo Alto, CA: Mayfield Publishing Company, 1984, pp. 267–75.

Silvera, Makeda. *Piece of My Heart: A Lesbian of Colour Anthology.* Toronto: Sister Vision Press, 1991.

Thompson, Karen and Julie Andrzejewski. *Why Can't Sharon Kowalski Come Home?* San Francisco: Spinsters/aunt lute, 1988.

Older Lesbians and Gay Men

Adelman, Marcy, PhD, editor. *Long Time Passing: Lives of Older Lesbians.* Boston: Alyson Publications, Inc., 1986.

Almvig, Chris. *The Invisible Minority: Aging and Lesbianism.* Utica, NY: Institute of Gerontology, Utica College of Syracuse, 1982.

"Aging Male Homosexual: Myth & Reality," *The Gerontologist,* August, 1977, vol. 17, pp. 328–32.

Berger, Raymond. "Rewriting a Bad Script: Older Lesbians and Gays." *Lesbian and Gay Issues: A Resource Manual for Social Workers,* edited by Hilda Hidalgo, Travis L. Peterson, Natalie Jane Woodman. Silver Spring, MD: National Association of Social Workers, Inc., 1985, pp. 53–59.

Berger, Raymond M. "Realities of Gay and Lesbian Aging." *Social Work,* January–February 1984, vol. 29, no. 1, pp. 57–62.

Berger, Raymond M. "The Unseen Minority: Older Gays and Lesbians." *Social Work,* May 1982, vol. 27, no. 3, pp. 236–42.

Fryer, Jonathan. *Isherwood: A Biography of Christopher Isherwood.* London: New England Library, 1977.

Furbank, Philip N. *E. M. Forster: A Life.* New York: Harcourt, Brace, Jovanovich, 1978.

Gidlow, Elsa. *Sapphic Songs: Eighteen to Eighty.* Mill Valley, CA: Druid Heights Books, 1982.

Hohson, Karen Green. "The Effects of Aging on Sexuality." *Health and Social Work,* 1984, pp. 25–35.

Kehoe, Monika. "The Hidden Sorority: Lesbians over 60." *On the IS-SUES,* vol. 12, 1989, pp. 22–24, 34.

———. *Lesbians Over 60 Speak For Themselves.* New York: Harrington Park Press, 1989.

Kelly, James. "Homosexuality and Aging." *Homosexual Behavior: A Modern Reappraisal,* edited by Judd Marmor. New York: Basic Books, 1980, pp. 176–93.

Kimmel, Douglas C. "Adult Development and Aging: Gay Perspective." *Journal of Social Issues,* Summer 1978, vol. 34, no. 3, pp. 113–30.

———. "Patterns of Aging Among Gay Men." *Christopher Street,* vol. 2, no. 5, 1977.

Laner, M. R. "Growing Older Male: Heterosexual and Homosexual." *The Gerontologist.* August 1978, vol. 18, pp. 496–501.

Laner, R. "Growing Older Female: Heterosexual and Homosexual." *Journal of Homosexuality,* Spring 1979, vol. 4, no. 3, p. 267.

Martin D. and P. Lyons. "The Older Lesbian." *Positively Gay*, edited by B. Berzon and R. Leighton. Millbrae, CA: Celestial Arts, 1979.

Porcino, J. *Growing Older, Getting Better: A Handbook for Women in the Second Half of Life*. New York, NY: Continuum, 1991

Rich, Adrienne C. *On Lies, Secrets, and Silence: Selected Prose. 1966–1978*. New York: W. W. Norton, 1979.

Sarton, M. *Recovering: A Journal*. New York: W. W. Norton and Company, 1986.

"Senior Action in a Gay Environment: SAGE." *Practice Digest*, Summer, 1984, vol. 7, no. 1, pp. 17–20.

Simpson, Marita and Martha Wheelock. *World of Light: A Portrait of May Sarton*. New York: Ishtar Enterprises, 1982 [Book, film, audiotape].

Vacha, Keith. *Quiet Fire: Memoirs of Older Gay Men*. Trumansburg, NY: The Crossing Press, 1985.

Religion

Boswell, John. *Christianity, Social Tolerance and Homosexuality*. Chicago and London: University of Chicago Press, 1987.

Curb, Rosemary & Nancy Manahan. *Lesbian Nuns: Breaking Silence: Their Moving True Stories of Courage, Struggle, and Change*. New York: Warner Books, 1985.

Denmin, Rosemary. *Let My People In: A Lesbian Minister Tells of Her Struggles to Live Openly and Maintain Her Ministry*. New York: William Morrow and Company, 1990.

Field, David. *The Homosexual Way—A Christian Option?* Downers Grove, IL: InterVarsity Press, 1979.

Hiltner, Seward. "Homosexuality and the Churches." *Homosexual Behavior: A Modern Reappraisal*, edited by Judd Marmor. New York: Basic Books, 1980, pp. 219–31.

Holy Bible. King James Version. New York: American Bible Society, 1987.

Lanphear, Roger. *Gay Spirituality: Experiences in Self-Realization*. California: Unified Publications, 1990.

McNeill, John J., S. J. *The Church and the Homosexual*. Kansas City: Sheed, Andrews, and McMeel, 1976.

———. *The Church and the Homosexual: Third Edition, Updated and Expanded*. Boston: Beacon Press, 1988.

———. *Taking a Chance On God: Liberating Theology For Gays, Lesbians, And Their Lovers, Families, and Friends*. Boston: Beacon Press, 1988.

Moore, Paul, Jr. *Take a Bishop Like Me*. New York: Harper and Row, 1979.

Nelson, James B., PhD. "Religious and Moral Issues in Working with Homosexual Clients." *A Guide to Psychotherapy with Gay and Lesbian*

Clients, edited by John C. Gonsiorek. New York: Harrington Park Press, 1985, pp. 163–75.

Perry, Troy. *The Lord Is My Shepherd And He Knows I'm Gay.* University Fellowship M.C.C., 5300 Santa Monica Boulevard, Los Angeles, CA 90029, 1972.

The United Church of Christ. *Human Sexuality: A Preliminary Study.* New York and Philadelphia: United Church Press, 1977.

Thompson, Mark. *Gay Spirit: Myth and Meaning.* New York: St. Martin's Press, 1987.

DeStefano, G. "Gay Drug Abuse." *The Advocate,* no. 449, June 24, 1986.

Substance Abuse

"Alcohol Awareness." *Our Voice,* edited by K. Deniston, vol. 4, no. 1, March 1989.

Anderson, S. C. and D. C. Henderson. "Working with Lesbian Alcoholics." *Social Work,* vol. 30, no. 6, 1985, pp. 518–25.

Blume, E. S. "Substance Abuse: Of Being Queer, Magic Pills, and Social Lubricants," in *Lesbian and Gay Issues: A Resource Manual for Social Workers,* edited by H. Hidalgo, T. L. Peterson, and N. J. Woodman. National Association of Social Workers, pp. 78–88.

Brandsma, M. M. and E. M. Pattison. "Homosexuality and Alcoholism," *Encyclopedic Handbook of Alcoholism,* edited by Pattison and E. Kaufman. New York: Gardner Press, 1982, pp. 736–41.

Faltz, Barbara, RN, MS. "Substance Abuse and the Lesbian and Gay Community: Assessment and Intervention," *The Sourcebook on Lesbian/Gay Health Care,* second edition, edited by Michael Shernoff, MSW, ACSW and William A. Scott, MSW, ACP. Washington, DC: National Lesbian/Gay Health Foundation, pp. 151–61.

Fifield, L. *On My Way To Nowhere: Alienated, Isolated, Drunk.* Los Angeles: Gay Community Services Center and Department of Health Services, 1975.

Finnegan, Dana G. and Emily B. McNally. *Dual Identities: Counseling Chemically Dependent Gay Men and Lesbians.* Center City, Minnesota: Hazelden, 1987.

———— and Emily B. McNally, MEd, CAC. "The Lonely Journey: Lesbians and Gay Men Who Are Co-Dependent," *The Sourcebook on Lesbian/Gay Health Care,* second edition, edited by Michael Shernoff, MSW, ACSW and William A. Scott, MSW, ACP, Washington, DC: National Lesbian/Gay Health Foundation, pp. 173–79.

Gay Council on Drinking Behavior. *The Way Back: The Stories of Gay and Lesbian Alcoholics.* Washington, DC: Whitman–Walker Clinic, 1982.

Kus, Robert J. RN, PhD. "Alcoholism and Non-Acceptance of Gay Self: The Critical Link," *Journal of Homosexuality,* vol. 15, nos. 1–2, 1988, pp. 25–41.

Lohrenz, L., Donnelly, J., Coyne, L. and K. Spare. "Alcohol Problems in Several Midwestern Homosexual Communities," *Journal of Studies on Alcohol*, vol. 39, 1978, pp. 1959–63.

Morales, E. S. and M. A. Graves. *Substance Abuse: Patterns and Barriers to Treatment for Gay Men and Lesbians in San Francisco.* San Francisco: Department of Public Health, Community Substance Abuse Services, 1983, pp. 16–25.

Nardi, P. M. "Alcoholism and Homosexuality: A Theoretical Perspective," *Journal of Homosexuality*, vol. 7, no. 4, pp. 9–25.

Pohl, Melvin I. MD. "Recovery from Alcoholism and Chemical Dependence for Lesbians and Gay Men," *The Sourcebook on Lesbian/Gay Health Care*, second edition, edited by Michael Shernoff, MSW, ACSW and William A. Scott, MSW, ACP. Washington, DC: National Lesbian/Gay Health Foundation, pp. 169–72.

Ratner, Ellen F. EdM. "Treatment Issues for Chemically Dependent Lesbians and Gay Men," *The Sourcebook on Lesbian/Gay Health Care*, second edition, edited by Michael Shernoff MSW, ACSW and William A. Scott, MSW, ACP, Washington, D.C.: National Lesbian/Gay Health Foundation, pp. 162–69.

Smith, T. M. "Specific Approaches and Techniques in the Treatment of Gay Male Alcohol Abusers," *Journal of Homosexuality*, vol. 7, no. 4, 1982, pp. 53–69.

Zehner, M. A. and J. Lewis. "Homosexuality and Alcoholism," *With Compassion Toward Some*, edited by R. Schoenberg, R. Goldberg, and D. Shore. New York: Harrington Park Press, pp. 75–90.

Ziebold, Thomas O. PhD. and John E. Mongeon, guest editors. *Alcoholism and Homosexuality*, vol. 7, no. 4, Summer 1982, pp. 1–103.

Ziebold, Thomas O., PhD. *Alcoholism in the Gay Community*, Washington, DC: Whitman–Walker Clinic and Blade Communications, 1978.

Copyright Acknowledgments

Every reasonable effort has been made to locate the owners of rights to previously published material printed here. The authors and publisher gratefully acknowledge permission from the following sources to print material in this book:

Alyson Publications, Inc., for portions from *Reflection of a Rock Lobster* by Aaron Fricke.

Daily Freeman, Kingston, New York, for quotes from the *Sunday Freeman,* June 25, 1989.

Family Service America as a source of information on family-related issues, for their definition of "family." Information Center, Family Service America, 11700 West Lake Park Drive, Milwaukee, WI 53224.

Harper & Row, Publishers, Inc., for permission to quote from *Take a Bishop Like Me* by Paul Moore, Jr. Copyright © 1979 by Paul Moore, Jr. Reprinted with permission of Harper & Row, Publishers, Inc.

Joan Nestle, Lesbian Herstory Archives, for permission to use material from unpublished diary reproduced in the *Lesbian Herstory Archives Newsletter,* no. 10, February 1988.

New York Native and Simmons Market Research for permission to use brief excerpts from the October 1988 reader profile, based on a survey performed by Simmons Market Research.

New York Times for permission to quote excerpts from the follow-

THE CROSSROAD COUNSELING LIBRARY
Books of Related Interest

James Archer, Jr.
COUNSELING COLLEGE STUDENTS
A Practical Guide for Teachers, Parents, and Counselors
"Must reading for everyone on campus—professors,
administrators, dorm personnel, chaplains, and friends—as
well as parents and other counselors to whom college students
turn for support."—*Dr. William Van Ornum* $17.95

Denyse Beaudet
ENCOUNTERING THE MONSTER
Pathways in Children's Dreams
Based on original empirical research, and with recourse to the
works of Jung, Neumann, Eliade, Marie-Louise Franz, and
others, this book offers proven methods of approaching and
understanding the dream life of children. $19.95

Robert W. Buckingham
CARE OF THE DYING CHILD
A Practical Guide for Those Who Help Others
"Buckingham's book delivers a powerful, poignant message
deserving a wide readership."—*Library Journal* $17.95

Sidney Callahan
PARENTS FOREVER
You and Your Adult Children
An award-winning writer, psychologist, and mother of six
adult children offers reassurance and wisdom to millions of
other parents who never knew it would go on for so long....
$19.95

Alastair V. Campbell, ed.
A DICTIONARY OF PASTORAL CARE
Provides information on the essentials of counseling and the
kinds of problems encountered in pastoral practice. The
approach is interdenominational and interdisciplinary.
Contains over 300 entries by 185 authors in the fields of
theology, philosophy, psychology, and sociology as well as
from the theoretical background of psychotherapy and
counseling. $24.50

David A. Crenshaw
BEREAVEMENT
Counseling the Grieving throughout the Life Cycle
Grief is examined from a life cycle perspective, infancy to old
age. Special losses and practical strategies for frontline
caregivers highlight this comprehensive guidebook.
$17.95 hardcover $10.95 paperback

Paul J. Curtin
HIDDEN RICHES
Stories of ACOAs on the Journey of Recovery
A book of hope and healing for every ACOA or for anyone
who knows and loves someone who grew up in a
dysfunctional family. $8.95 paperback

Paul J. Curtin
TUMBLEWEEDS
A Therapist's Guide to Treatment of ACOAs
A book for those who are ACOAs and for those who wish to
help ACOAs in their search to experience and share themselves
honestly. $7.95 paperback

Paul J. Curtin
RESISTANCE AND RECOVERY
For Adult Children of Alcoholics
The ideal companion to *Tumbleweeds, Resistance and Recovery*
shows how resistance is vital and necessary to recovery when
obstacles are turned into growth opportunities.
$7.95 paperback

Eugene Kennedy
SEXUAL COUNSELING
A Practical Guide for Those Who Help Others
Newly revised and up-to-date edition of an essential book on
counseling people with sexual problems, with a new chapter
on the counselor and AIDS. $17.95

Judith M. Knowlton
HIGHER POWERED
A Ninety Day Guide to Serenity and Self-Esteem
"A treasure! Not only those in recovery, but everyone seeking
peace and self-assurance will benefit from the ideas and
inspiration in this excellent book."—*Thomas W. Perrin*
$9.95 paperback

Bonnie Lester
WOMEN AND AIDS
A Practical Guide for Those Who Help Others
Provides positive ways for women to deal with their fears, and
to help others who react with fear to people who have AIDS.
$15.95

Robert J. Lovinger
RELIGION AND COUNSELING
The Psychological Impact of Religious Belief
How counselors and clergy can best understand the important
emotional significance of religious thoughts and feelings.
$17.95

Sophie L. Lovinger, Mary Ellen Brandell, and
Linda Seestedt-Stanford
LANGUAGE LEARNING DISABILITIES
*A New and Practical Approach for Those Who Work with Children
and Their Families*
Here is new information, together with practical suggestions,
on how teachers, therapists, and families can work together to
give learning disabled children new strengths. $22.95

Helen B. McDonald and Audrey I. Steinhorn
UNDERSTANDING HOMOSEXUALITY
A Guide for Those Who Know, Love, or Counsel Gay and Lesbian Individuals
A sensitive guide to better understanding and counseling gay men, lesbians, and their parents, at every stage of their lives.
$10.95 paperback

James McGuirk and Mary Elizabeth McGuirk
FOR WANT OF A CHILD
A Psychologist and His Wife Explore the Emotional Effects and Challenges of Infertility
A new understanding of infertility that comes from one couple's lived experience, as well as sound professional advice for couples and counselors. $14.95

Janice N. McLean and Sheila A. Knights
PHOBICS AND OTHER PANIC VICTIMS
A Practical Guide for Those Who Help Them
"A must for the phobic, spouse and family, and for the physician and support people who help them."—*Arthur B. Hardy, M. D., Founder, TERRAP Phobia Program* $17.95

John B. Mordock and William Van Ornum
CRISIS COUNSELING WITH CHILDREN AND ADOLESCENTS
A Guide for Nonprofessional Counselors
New Expanded Edition
"Every parent should keep this book on the shelf right next to the nutrition, medical, and Dr. Spock books."—*Marriage & Family Living* $12.95

John B. Mordock
COUNSELING CHILDREN
Basic Principles for Helping the Troubled and Defiant Child
Helps counselors consider the best route for a particular child, and offers proven principles and methods to counsel troubled children in a variety of situations. $17.95

John R. Shack
COUPLES COUNSELING
A Practical Guide for Those Who Help Others
An essential guide to dealing with the 20 percent of all
counseling situations that involve a relationship. $15.95

Milton F. Shore, Patrick J. Brice, and Barbara G. Love
WHEN YOUR CHILD NEEDS TESTING
*What Parents, Teachers, and Other Helpers Need to Know about
Psychological Testing*
A helpful map to the world of psychological testing that will
ease fears and encourage better decision making among
parents and others who care for children and adolescents.
$18.95

Herbert S. Strean as told to Lucy Freeman
BEHIND THE COUCH
Revelations of a Psychoanalyst
"An entertaining account of an analyst's thoughts and
feelings."—*Psychology Today* $11.95 paperback

Stuart Sutherland
THE INTERNATIONAL DICTIONARY OF PSYCHOLOGY
This new dictionary of psychology also covers a wide range of
related disciplines, from anthropology to sociology. $49.50

Joan Leslie Taylor
IN THE LIGHT OF DYING
The Journals of a Hospice Volunteer
"Beautifully recounts the healing (our own) that results from
service to others, and might well be considered as required
reading for hospice volunteers."—Stephen Levine, author of
Who Dies? $17.95

William Van Ornum and Mary W. Van Ornum
TALKING TO CHILDREN ABOUT NUCLEAR WAR
"A wise book. A needed book. An urgent book."
—*Dr. Karl A. Menninger*
$14.95 hardcover $9.95 paperback